Belle  Bob
La Follette

Other Badger Biographies

Bob & Belle La Follette

Partners in Politics

Bob Kann

Wisconsin Historical Society Press

Published by the Wisconsin Historical Society Press
Publishers since 1855

© 2008 by State Historical Society of Wisconsin

Publication of this book was made possible, in part, by a gift from Mrs. Harvey E. Vick of Milwaukee, Wisconsin.

www.wisconsinhistory.org

Photographs identified with PH, WHi, or WHS are from the Society's collections; address inquiries about such photos to the Visual Materials Archivist at Wisconsin Historical Society, 816 State Street, Madison, WI 53706.

Printed in Wisconsin, U.S.A
Designed by Jill Bremigan

12 11 10 09 08   1 2 3 4 5

Library of Congress Cataloging-in-Publication Data

Kann, Bob.
  Belle and Bob La Follette : partners in politics / by Bob Kann.
      p. cm.—(Badger biographies)
  Includes bibliographical references and index.
  ISBN 978-0-87020-407-4 (pbk. : alk. paper)
1. La Follette, Robert M. (Robert Marion), 1855-1925—Juvenile literature. 2. La Follette, Belle Case, 1859-1931—Juvenile literature. 3. Legislators—United States—Biography—Juvenile literature. 4. United States. Congress. Senate—Biography—Juvenile literature. 5. Progressivism (United States politics) —Juvenile literature. 6. Politicians—Wisconsin—Biography—Juvenile literature. 7. Social reformers—Wisconsin—Biography—Juvenile literature. 8. Married people—Wisconsin—Biography—Juvenile literature. 9. Wisconsin—Politics and government—1848-1950—Juvenile literature. 10. Wisconsin—Social policy—Juvenile literature. I. Title.
  E664.L16K36 2008
  973.09'9—dc22
                            2008004312

Front cover: Belle and Bob La Follette in 1925, WHi Image ID 10739. Back cover: Bob La Follette in 1900, WHi Image ID 10900; Belle Case La Follete in 1905, WHi Image ID 30384.

∞ The paper used in this publication meets the minimum requirements of the American National Standard for Information Sciences—Permanence of Paper for Printed Library Materials, ANSI Z39.48-1992.

Contents

1

Meet Belle and Bob

What would it take to do something in your lifetime that would help people in the future?

In Wisconsin **politics**, there is no more famous couple than the La Follettes. Belle and Bob **La Follette**, who lived 100 years ago, believed that making a better world is both good and possible.

By 1900, the huge growth of factories and businesses had caused many problems in the United States. A small group of men possessed much of the wealth and power in the country. Many **politicians** were dishonest. There was a great deal of **poverty**. Young children worked in factories and mines. As people became aware of these problems, a desire for **reform** swept the country.

politics: the way a city, state, or nation governs itself   **La Follette** (luh **fah** let)   **politician** (pol uh **tish** un): someone who runs for or holds public office, such as a senator   **poverty**: the state of being poor
reform: changing something for the better

The La Follettes became 2 leaders of the reform **movement**. Together, they fought for issues that are still important today: taking care of the poor, making sure everyone has the same **rights**, and getting rid of dishonest politicians. Bob and Belle were unusual because they were equal partners in Bob's

WHI IMAGE ID 5455

Bob La Follette was well-known for his fiery, persuasive speeches.

political work. Many men of the time did not consider women to be their equals, but Bob depended upon Belle's advice as he made important decisions.

Bob held many political **offices** during his lifetime. He was a governor, a congressman, and a senator. Bob was honest and fearless. He had a special kind of courage that earned him the nickname "Fighting Bob." He fought stubbornly for the

movement: a group of people who have joined together to support a cause   **right**: a thing you are allowed to do or have by law, such as going to school or being able to vote   **office**: a political job, such as governor, senator, or president

2

causes he believed in, and he rarely backed down. He was an outstanding, **persuasive** speaker, full of energy when he spoke in front of a large crowd. People from Wisconsin voted for him again and again.

Belle's wisdom, intelligence, and care for his health helped Bob to succeed as a politician. She supported Bob in many of his causes, but she also fought for her own causes, such as world peace and women being able to vote. Belle didn't listen when people said women shouldn't take part in **public affairs**. She gave speeches, wrote articles, and even got a law degree! With Bob, she raised 4 children. Two of them also became famous politicians.

This book tells the tale of Bob and Belle La Follette and how they fought for a better **society**. This political couple shared dreams and goals that bound them together in a love story that lasted for more than 40 years. Read their story to find out how 2 farm kids from Wisconsin changed the world.

---

persuasive (pur **sway** siv): good at giving reasons for someone to believe something   **public affairs**: issues that affect everybody, such as health or education   **society**: all the people who live in the same country and share the same laws or customs

2

I Don't Hate to Do Anything
That Needs to Be Done

In the early-morning hours of April 21, 1859, a newborn baby's cry rang out. That baby's name was Belle. Her parents, Mary and Anson Case, lived in a log cabin in Summit, Wisconsin, far from the hospitals and clinics where most babies are born

today. In 1859, it wasn't at all unusual for a baby to be born at home. On that early spring morning, Mary and Anson could not have imagined their daughter would one day be married to a famous politician, or that she would be the first woman in Wisconsin to go to **law school.**

Belle, age 6, is wearing a dress woven and sewn by her Grandmother Case.

law school: a school one attends to learn to be a lawyer

4

In 1862, when Belle was 3, she moved with her parents and her older brother Roy to Baraboo, Wisconsin, where she would spend the rest of her childhood. Her parents moved because they wanted to be closer to Anson's parents, Archibald and

Belle was born in a cabin like this in Summit, Wisconsin, in 1859.

Lucetta Case. They also wanted to raise **hops**, a popular crop in the Baraboo area. Farming was hard, backbreaking work. Anson and Mary had to work long hours to make their farm

a success. Because they were often busy, Belle spent a lot of time with her grandmother, Lucetta Case. Grandma Case loved being with her granddaughter.

Like this young girl, Belle grew up on a farm that produced crops such as wheat and hops.

hops: the dried, ripe flowers of the hop plant, which contains a bitter oil used in making beer

Grandma Case had little schooling because her mother died when she was 10 years old. She became responsible for looking out for her younger brothers and sisters and for taking care of the family's home. However, she was intelligent and taught herself many things that she later passed on to her granddaughter. Belle wrote, "Even as a child I wondered what there was that my grandmother did not know. She knew the Bible and had **absorbed** not only the spiritual lessons, but its **choice** English. She was in close touch with nature; she could name the **constellations** and tell time by the stars. She could make beautiful vegetable dyes and knew the **medicinal** use of herbs."

Grandma Case was always busy with her hands, sewing and weaving clothing. Belle loved the checkered wool dress and **Balmoral** skirt Grandma Case made for her. "They were so long," she said, "I could not forget them." One day, when she and Belle were sewing rags together to make carpets, Belle asked whether Grandma Case hated doing a task that took such a long

absorbed (uhb **zorbd**): taken in, understood   **choice**: well chosen, of good quality   **constellation** (kahn stuh **lay** shun): a group of stars that forms a shape or pattern   **medicinal** (me **di** si nuhl): used to treat illness **Balmoral** (bahl **maw** ruhl): Scottish

time. "No, child," she answered, "I don't hate to do anything that needs to be done."

Belle learned to work hard from her parents and from Grandma Case, but it wasn't farmwork or household chores that she liked best. The place where Belle shined was in the schoolroom. Belle attended a country school near

Belle's grandmother, Lucetta Case.

her grandmother's farm. No matter how bad the weather, she walked 2 miles each way. She was never late and rarely

Belle attended grades 1 through 12 in a one-room schoolhouse like this one.

absent during the 12 years she attended. The only time she missed school was when she was sick with the measles.

Belle's hard work and intelligence did not go unnoticed. In June 1875, at the age of 16, she graduated from high school at the top of her class. Girls, particularly farm girls, rarely went to college during the 1870s. The University of Wisconsin had only recently begun to allow girls to attend the same classes boys had been attending for several **decades**. Fortunately, Belle's grandmother was **determined** that Belle should receive the education that she herself never had. Belle's parents also saw that their daughter deserved to go to college and have the chance to choose her own path. They wanted Belle to be able to do whatever she set her mind to.

Mary and Anson saved money for her education, and in 1875 Belle moved to Madison to attend the University of Wisconsin, 30 miles from her home in Baraboo. Belle did not disappoint her parents. She studied hard and was an excellent student. And there she soon met the love of her life, Bob La Follette.

decade (**dek** ayd): a period of 10 years   **determined**: absolutely sure

3
My Name Is La Follette

On June 14, 1855, a baby boy was born to Josiah and Mary La Follette. They named him Robert, but everyone called him Bob. Like Belle, Bob was born in a log cabin. His parents had moved to Wisconsin in a **covered wagon** several years earlier. They lived in the town of Primrose, 25 miles from Madison. Legend has it that Bob's aunts and uncles grew up playing with young Abraham Lincoln—after all, they had grown up next to the Lincoln farm in Kentucky before his father, Josiah, was born.

An 1858 portrait of Mary La Follette and her children, Bob, Josephine, William, and Ellen (standing).

Josiah and Mary La Follette's cabin was near a **spring** on a piece of land that was mostly **prairie**. The home had a

covered wagon: a large, wooden wagon with a canvas cover spread over metal hoops, used by pioneers in the 1800s
spring: a place where water rises up from underground and becomes a stream **prairie** (**prair** ee): a large area of flat or rolling grassland with few or no trees

stove, an oven, a cellar, and something unusual for the times, a bookcase filled with books. One of those books, *Lives of the Presidents of the United States*, may have planted a seed of interest in young Bob. Perhaps it made

A drawing of the cabin where Bob was born in Primrose, Wisconsin, in 1855.

him think that someday he might become president.

Eight months after Bob was born, his father died of **pneumonia**, leaving Mary and her 4 children to cope with life on the Wisconsin **frontier**. Bob was too young to remember his father, but as soon as he was old enough to understand, his mother taught him that he must never do anything to **disgrace** his father's name. Like his father, he must be honest and do what was right. Throughout his life, Bob would be known for his honesty and for his loyalty to the La Follette name.

Bob's honesty was tested early in his life. When he was 5 years old, Bob found a **pocketbook** in the road that he took

pneumonia (nuh **mohn** yuh): a disease that causes the lungs to be filled with fluid, making breathing difficult
frontier: the far edge of a settled area, where few people live   **disgrace**: to cause shame or embarrassment
pocketbook: a small case used to hold money

home and gave to his mother. The next morning, the man who had lost the pocketbook was able to get it back, thanks to Bob's honesty. He rewarded Bob with 25 cents. It was the first money Bob had ever earned. He had a hole drilled into the coin and wore it around his neck like a medal.

Bob was sad when Abraham Lincoln was killed in 1865.

Bob grew up during the **Civil War**. Like other boys, he played soldier, dressing up and marching around like the men he'd seen leave for battle. But Bob learned that war wasn't always about glory. His teacher was killed in battle. And Bob remembered the moment when a neighbor told him that President Lincoln had been **assassinated**.

Civil War soldiers.

Civil War: the war between the Southern states and the Northern states over the issue of slavery, which lasted from 1861 to 1865   **assassinated** (uh **sa** si nay tud): killed because of fame or power

He ran home to tell his mother, and the whole family cried.

WHI IMAGE ID 30156

Like Belle's family, Bob's mother, Mary, strongly believed in the value of education. Bob started to attend school in Primrose when he was only 4 years old, although he had to walk almost a mile up and down many hills. The school in Primrose was a typical country schoolhouse. It had only one room with one teacher who taught all subjects to more than 100 students! Like many country schools, it went up to only the eighth grade.

Bob La Follette at age 9.

Even before he started school, Bob learned how to perform for an audience. When he was just 3 years old, he was lifted onto the teacher's desk in the newly built Primrose schoolhouse and cried: "You'd **scarce** expect one of my age to speak upon the public stage." This was a common **recitation** for children. Later in his life, Bob would become famous for his public speeches.

scarce: hardly recitation (re si **tay** shun): a speech that is memorized and performed

When Bob was 7, an important event occurred in his family. His mother married a man named John Saxton. Saxton wasn't the kind of stepfather Bob had hoped for. Saxton was strict and often whipped Bob when he misbehaved. Saxton's cruel discipline made Bob angry. Even as a little boy, Bob would correct anyone who called him Bob Saxton. He'd insist, "My name is La Follette."

Despite his fear of Saxton, Bob often got into trouble. One winter day, he and his friends, Charlie Pullen and Perry Wilder, pried loose a large chunk of ice from the **Pecatonica** River and climbed on top. Much to their surprise, their "ice boat" began floating down the river. Before they knew it, they had drifted several miles downstream! Bob later said that "my stepfather made it as hot for me when he got home as it had been cold on the ice raft."

From the ages of 13 to 15, Bob lived at a **boarding house** in Argyle, Wisconsin, a town near Primrose, so that he could go to the school there. In Argyle, Bob had to earn his own money for food and clothing. After school each day, he worked as a

Pecatonica: pek uh **tah** nik uh   **boarding house**: a house that provided meals and rooms for students living away from home

13

Bob, in the center, lived with these boys while he attended school in Argyle, Wisconsin.

barber cutting hair in a local hotel. Bob was very concerned about his appearance, so styling hair was a good job for him. He'd already begun to wear his hair in a **pompadour** style, partly because it made him look taller. He would grow to be only 5 feet 6 inches tall. As an adult, he would be well known for this hairstyle.

In 1870, when Bob was 15 years old, his stepfather became ill. Bob moved back to Primrose to help **manage** the family farm. Belle later wrote, "There was no work on a farm Bob could not do well. He plowed a straight **furrow** and plowed deep. He handled a **scythe** with

pompadour (**pom** puh dor): a hairstyle in which the front hair is swept up from the forehead **manage**: to be in charge of something **furrow**: the groove cut by a plow when it turns over the soil **scythe** (sIth): a tool with a large curved blade used for cutting grass or crops by hand

14

an ease and rhythm delightful to watch. He knew how the crops should be planted, the **stock** cared for, how the haying, harvesting, and all the things that are a part of

Bob's first love was working the land.

the day's work on the farm should be done." For 2 years, Bob poured all of his energy into the farm. When his stepfather died in 1872, Bob took on more responsibility for the farm.

Most of the grain, butter, eggs, and chickens from the Primrose farm were sold at the market in Madison. It took a team of horses a whole day to travel over the dirt roads to complete the 24-mile journey. Farmers such as Bob would leave home the day before the market day so they could reach the **Gorham** House, a few miles outside of Madison, before it got dark. They would spend the night at Gorham House, rise early the next morning to sell their goods, and then return

stock: cows, horses, pigs, and other animals raised on a farm   **Gorham: gor** uhm

home the same day. The money Bob earned from these sales was very important to his family.

Bob continued to work on the farm until he was 19 years old. That's when his mother sold the farm so that Bob could attend the University of Wisconsin. The La Follettes filled a wagon with furniture. They climbed aboard, and Bob's horse, **Gypsy**, pulled them all the way to Madison. The family cow trailed behind the wagon attached by a rope. They moved into a house Bob had rented on the edge of town, which had a barn and a pasture. Although Bob's days as a farmer were over, the values of hard work, independence, and honesty he gained during his early years would remain with him for the rest of his life.

Gypsy: jip see

4

Mama Laughed When I Proposed to Her

In 1875, both Belle and Bob entered the **University** of Wisconsin (UW) in Madison. At that time, the university had a total of 345 students, and there were fewer than 27,000 college students in the entire United States. In 2008, there are more than 40,000 students attending the UW.

This is what the University of Wisconsin looked like when Belle and Bob were students. Classes are still held in many of these buildings today.

University: yoo nuh **vur** suh tee

When Belle arrived in Madison for school, it was the first time she had visited such a large city. Madison, the **state capital**, was the second largest city in Wisconsin. It had twice as many people as Baraboo, her hometown. How exciting and scary this big city must have been for a girl who grew up on a farm! In 1871, the university opened its first **dormitory** for women, Ladies Hall. Belle lived there from 1875 to 1879. Ladies Hall had an "indoor **privy**," a plumbing invention that first came to Madison in 1855.

Most students who attended the UW in the 1870s were boys who came from farms just as Bob had. They saw college as an opportunity to have careers in law, medicine, and business. Yet when he moved to Madison to go to college, Bob had no idea what he wanted to do with his degree.

Like many students, Bob worked at a variety of jobs to support himself and his family. His first job was selling books by going door-to-door to houses in Madison. He always sold a handheld mirror along with the books. When "the lady of the house" opened the door, he'd have the mirror ready so

state capital: the city where the state government is located   **dormitory**: a building with many rooms for sleeping
privy (prI vee): a toilet

18

that she could see her face. He figured this would naturally make her friendlier to the bookseller. Bob's mother and sister also helped to pay for Bob's education by cooking meals and renting rooms in their

Bob's mother, Mary, kept a boarding house in Madison for boys attending the University of Wisconsin.

house for 20 boys who were also attending the university.

For 2 years before he started at the university, Bob had to attend a special school, the Wisconsin Classical and **Commercial** Academy. It was common for boys and girls who had attended country schools to require extra schooling after high school to be ready for the university. During the fall of 1873, Bob attended classes at night and worked during the day.

In 1875, both Belle and Bob started their **freshman year** at the university. It wasn't long before the 2 met for the

Commercial: kuh **mur** shuhl   **freshman year**: the first year of college

A college dormitory room from 100 years ago.

very first time in their German class. One day the teacher, Miss Carver, scolded a group of young men who were **disrupting** the lesson. One young man, Robert La Follette, caught Belle's eye. She saw that Bob was "the **prime** cause of the mischief." He would play many jokes over their years together.

Belle and Bob liked each other immediately. They discovered that they shared many things. They both came from farms. They both loved to learn, and they both wanted to make the world a better place. They also loved to laugh.

At the end of their **junior year**, Bob asked Belle to marry him. At first, Belle was unsure. She wanted to keep their

disrupting: disturbing or interrupting   **prime**: main   **junior year**: the third year of college

friendship light, and she even questioned whether Bob was serious. After all, he had played many jokes on her. Later, Bob would tell their children, "Mama laughed when I **proposed** to her." Belle explained to them, "If I did, it was Papa's fault. He had been so **disposed** to make me laugh when I was in his company, how could I be sure he was not joking?" Belle finally agreed to marry Bob, but she insisted that they keep their engagement a secret until they both had graduated.

For Belle and Bob, the college years were busy but exciting. Belle quickly gained a **reputation** for being an excellent student. Just like in the country school in Baraboo, she rarely missed a day. She graduated near the top of her class. Two of her teachers, Professor Carpenter and Professor Olin, told her that she was a talented writer and should consider writing as a career, but Belle lacked **confidence** in her writing abilities. She later wished she had listened to their advice. At the end of her life, she said, "I did not take these suggestions as seriously then as I would if I were beginning over again."

proposed: asked someone to marry you   **disposed**: ready   **reputation** (rep yoo **tay** shun): your worth or character, as judged by other people   **confidence**: strong belief in oneself or one's abilities

21

Bob continued to work throughout his college years. He cut hair and also taught classes in a country school in the town of Burke. He rode his horse, Gypsy, 5 miles each day to and from the school. His most successful project began in 1876 when he borrowed $400 from a friend to buy the college newspaper, the *University Press*. Within one year, he made the paper so successful that it had earned $700. He also doubled the number of pages in the newspaper from 4 pages to 8.

Managing the newspaper was a huge responsibility, and it took up a great deal of his time. But Bob loved running his own paper. He was especially good at selling newspaper ads to local stores with his **slogan**, "He who is wise, will advertise." Bob worked day and night, gathering college news, writing **reviews** of plays, and printing **essays** by professors.

Because so much of his time was spent at the paper and not in class, Bob gained a reputation for being a poor student. He did, however, pay special attention to the **lectures** delivered on Sundays by university president John Bascom. President Bascom encouraged students to think for themselves and turn

slogan: a phrase or motto   **review**: a piece of writing that gives an opinion about a new book, play, or movie
essay: a piece of writing about a particular subject   **lecture** (**lek** shur): a talk given to an audience, often at a college or university

their beliefs into actions. He encouraged
them to "do right" and to serve the public.
These messages helped guide Bob's
thoughts and behaviors for the rest of
his life. Belle agreed with Dr. Bascom's
ideas, too. Together, she and Bob **vowed**
that whatever they did, they would work
to make the world a better place.

University president John
Bascom influenced Belle and
Bob to make the world a better
place.

　　Early in their friendship, Belle and
Bob began to help each other. Belle
helped Bob with his studies, and Bob helped Belle with her
speeches for class. During their junior and senior year, each
student was required to give an **oration**. When Belle gave her
oration, she became so nervous that she couldn't remember
a single word. She returned to her seat in shame. She was
embarrassed and felt as though she had failed. Her professor
told her that to pass the class she'd have to give a new
speech. Bob helped her practice before her second try. With
his help, she recited her speech without a single mistake.

vowed: promised　**oration** (or **ay** shun): a memorized speech given in front of an audience

Unlike Belle, Bob loved to perform in front of an audience. Bob acted in many plays while at the university, often playing the lead role. He thought seriously about a career in acting. When the great actor John **McCullough** came to Madison, Bob asked him to **evaluate** his acting talent. McCullough told Bob that because he was only 5 and a half feet tall, he was too short to play a leading man or a **villain** and should think about

WHI IMAGE ID 47266

a different profession. Bob followed this advice and gave up his dream of becoming an actor. Even so, his skills on the stage were helpful in later years when he became a public speaker and politician.

Although he chose not to become an actor, Bob loved performing in plays during college. Here, students perform a Japanese wedding.

The most important event for Bob during his **senior year** was the Interstate **Oratorical** Contest. In this contest, the best college speakers from 6 states competed to see who could give the most powerful and convincing speech. Bob was an excellent speaker. He could express ideas clearly, and he

McCullough: muh **ku** luh   **evaluate** (ee **val** yoo ayt): to decide how good or valuable something is after thinking carefully about it   **villain**: a wicked person, often an evil character in a play   **senior year**: the final year of college   **oratorical** (or uh **tor** i kul): having to do with public speaking

24

loved being in front of a crowd. When he prepared a speech, he chose each word and **gesture** carefully. He rehearsed again and again until he felt that he had it "just right."

On May 7, 1879, Bob traveled to Iowa City to perform in the Interstate Oratorical Contest. That night, 1,400 people jammed the city's opera house to hear the best speeches from 6 states. When Bob was announced as the winner, word spread quickly. Back in Madison, hundreds of students celebrated by dancing around a huge bonfire on the campus baseball field until after midnight. The next afternoon, another huge crowd of students greeted Bob at the train station to celebrate his triumph. Even a brass band came along! A party was held that evening in the state capitol building. Bob was honored as a state hero.

One month after Bob's success, Belle and Bob graduated from the university. But Bob almost didn't graduate. During the 1870s, all of the professors would gather together each June to decide which students were ready to receive their **diploma**. In most cases, they voted **unanimously** for each student. In Bob's case, however, there was a lot to talk about.

gesture (**jes** chur): a movement that shows a feeling   **diploma**: a certificate from a school showing that one has graduated   **unanimously** (yoo **nan** i muhs lee): with everyone's agreement

25

Belle and Bob's college graduation pictures.

Many professors felt he should not get his degree because he was a poor student and had failed many classes. Others argued that his work on the student newspaper and as an orator made up for his poor performance in classes. The discussion ended in a tied vote. University president John Bascom was asked to vote to break the tie. Without hesitation, President Bascom decided that Bob would graduate.

Unlike Bob, Belle turned out to be such an excellent student that she was one of the 16 students chosen to speak at the graduation ceremony. A prize would be awarded to the student whose oration was judged the best. Belle wrote her speech about what she had learned in her science class about the natural world. In the class, she had studied **corals**, **sea urchins**, and starfish, describing what she saw in detail. The experience taught her what it meant to really "see" something. Belle wrote, "I was amazed how little I knew of the art of seeing." She called her speech "Learning to See." With Bob's suggestions, Belle practiced and practiced. But she did not have much confidence that she would win. Bob, however, expected her to win the prize.

Bob's confidence in Belle was proved right. She spoke so well that she took first place! "I was so greatly pleased when it was awarded me," she later remembered. She was especially proud that her parents were there for her speech. "I remember seeing their faces while I was speaking," she wrote. "I was happy most of all for their sakes to hear the applause that followed the judge's decision."

coral: a rock-hard substance found underwater, made up of the skeletons of tiny sea creatures **sea urchin**: a small sea creature with a soft body enclosed by a hard, spiny shell

5

The Brainiest Member of the Family

Although they talked about getting married after college, Belle and Bob did not wed immediately after graduation. They wanted to save money for their life together, and they needed to make important decisions about the future. Before they graduated, Belle and Bob had talked about what career Bob might choose. With such excellent skills at making speeches, it seemed likely he would succeed at law. When he was a college student, Bob went to the courthouse whenever important cases were tried. He learned a great deal by watching Madison's best lawyers in action. The couple agreed that Bob would study law and Belle would teach school. Then, sometime in the future, they would buy their own farm and start a family.

While Bob stayed at the university to go to law school, Belle found a job as a teacher and assistant principal 30 miles from Madison at Spring Green High School. Belle greatly admired her high school students. Some were teachers themselves! In the 1880s, teachers weren't required to finish high school. Often, their education ended after eighth grade because there weren't a lot of high schools except in large towns. They were eager to learn more so that they could better teach their students. Belle said her students were there "because they were eager for an education. They were paying **tuition**, more often than not with money they had earned themselves." Until 1880, when the government started to provide high school education for free, many students had to pay for school. Belle worked hard to keep ahead of her students. She liked teaching, enjoyed living on her own, and took pride in her work.

Bob rode the train from Madison to Spring Green to visit Belle as often as he could. During one of these visits, he challenged Belle to a race "right in the village street." It is unknown who won the race, but Belle did say that she was a fast runner!

tuition (too i shun): money paid to take classes

The following year, Belle took a new job as a teacher in her hometown of Baraboo. Bob often would ride his horse, Gypsy, for 5 hours each way to visit his bride-to-be. This time Belle taught seventh grade. For their first assignment, she asked the class to write an essay. She remembered one tall boy named John Ringling was "good-natured, full of fun but had little taste for lessons or books." When he read his essay about the circus **sideshows** he and his brothers had been giving every night, his classmates laughed. Instead of complimenting his first essay, Belle told him to take his lessons more seriously.

After college, Belle worked as a teacher at this high school in Baraboo, Wisconsin.

In later years, Belle felt badly about **scolding** John for his essay. "Fortunately," she later wrote, "the scolding had no effect." Soon after, he and his older brothers started a small circus with musicians, clowns, a ringmaster, animals, and an

sideshow: a small performance that is part of a larger performance, such as at a circus   **scolding**: reprimanding, punishing

animal trainer. This was the beginning of Ringling Brothers Circus, which became one of the most famous circuses in the world.

One of Belle's students, John Ringling, started the Ringling Brothers Circus.

Meanwhile, Bob had started to attend the University of Wisconsin Law School, where he would study to become a lawyer. He received even more training in a Madison lawyer's office. While most students studied law for 2 years before taking the **bar exam**, Bob studied for only 7 months. He passed the exam and became a lawyer on February 5, 1880.

On December 31, 1881, Belle and Bob were married in Belle's family home in Baraboo. In the typical marriage ceremony of the day, the woman promised to "obey" her husband, while the man promised to "**cherish**" or love his wife.

bar exam: a test to see whether someone is ready to be a lawyer **cherish** (**chair** ish): to care for someone or something in a kind and loving way

Before they were married, Belle did something unusual for the times. She asked that the word *obey* be taken out of their marriage **vows**. She thought it was unfair that she would have to promise to obey Bob, but he wouldn't have to make the same promise to her. Bob agreed. He believed that Belle and he should be equal partners. After their wedding, Bob and Belle moved into the large house they bought

Bob and Belle lived in this house on West Wilson Street in Madison until Bob became governor in 1901.

on West Wilson Street in Madison. They shared the house with Bob's mother, his sister Mary, and her husband, Robert **Siebecker**.

Bob soon showed Belle how serious he was about becoming an excellent lawyer. During their first year of marriage, he spent his evenings at home reading law books. Belle joined him reading those books. When problems arose in his cases, they worked together reading the law books to

vow: a serious and important promise   **Siebecker**: **see** be kur

find solutions. But working hard also had a harmful effect on Bob. Shortly after they were married, Belle learned that her husband suffered from a variety of illnesses. At times he was **depressed**, and often he had stomachaches. He often tried to do too many things at the same time, and he would work so hard that he'd collapse from **fatigue**. Belle would care for Bob's health throughout their lives.

On September 10, 1882, Belle gave birth to a daughter, Flora, whom they nicknamed Fola. After her daughter was born, Belle said, "I was profoundly happy. I experienced wonderful contentment and restfulness of spirit. I believe the **supreme** experience in life is motherhood, yet I'm sure

Belle with the couple's first daughter, Fola, who was born in 1882.

depressed (dee **presd**): in a state of long-lasting unhappiness fatigue (fuh **teeg**): great tiredness
supreme: best, greatest

there is no **conflict** in a mother's taking good care of her children and developing her talents." She believed a woman could be a good mother and develop many other skills at the same time.

Belle wasted no time in developing her talents. Her work with Bob had **sparked** a serious interest in law. She said she "found it keenly enjoyable, quite different from any other studying I have done." She enrolled in UW's law school in the fall of 1883. This satisfied many of her needs. Law school challenged her curious mind. Studying law made her better able to understand and **counsel** her husband. As always, Belle proved to be an excellent student. In 1885, she became the first woman to graduate from the University of Wisconsin Law School. Belle never practiced law in a courtroom, but that didn't bother her. Developing her talents was important, and her law degree made her better able to support Bob's work.

Bob was also busy with his own career. In the fall of 1880, just 6 months after he became a lawyer, he made an

conflict: a problem or disagreement between 2 things   **sparked**: started   **counsel**: to give advice

important decision. He decided to run for **district attorney** of Dane County. A district attorney, or DA, is the lawyer who **represents** the city or county against people who commit crimes. The DA decides which cases should be tried in court. As DA, Bob would play an important role in fighting crime in Madison.

Bob's first election was a success. He was elected as district attorney in 1881 and again in 1882. For Bob, being elected as DA was the first step in becoming a powerful politician. It helped his reputation, and it gave him practice for bigger jobs, such as being a governor or senator. It also helped him to understand what it takes to win an election.

When Bob first ran for the office of district attorney in Dane County, he was confident that he would win. He had lived his entire life in Dane County, and he could count on the support of many of his friends. His victory at the Interstate Oratorical Contest in college had made him even more popular. He had learned to speak a little Norwegian as a boy, because many of his playmates and their families were from Norway.

district attorney (dis trikt uh **tur** nee): the lawyer who puts people on trial for crimes in a city or county
represents (rep ri **zents**): stands or acts for

Bob thought his ability to speak the language of many of the Norwegians who lived in Dane County would help him win the election.

Bob hitched up his horse, Gypsy, to a **buggy** and **campaigned** throughout the countryside. It was harvest time, so he'd visit with farmers in the fields during the day and in their homes during the evenings. He'd spend the night in one farmer's home and move on to another farm the next day. Bob's hard work paid off. The election was close: he won by only 93 votes!

Bob worked hard to gain the votes of local farmers, like those pictured here.

buggy: a carriage with 2 wheels, pulled by a horse   campaigned (cam **paynd**): talked with people and gave speeches in order to get votes

Guilty or Not Guilty?

When he became district attorney, Bob had not had much experience in the courtroom. This led to an embarrassing moment during his very first case. At the beginning of the hearing, the judge asked Bob if the person accused of the crime had been "**arraigned**." Bob did not know that arraigned meant to ask the person accused of the crime to say whether he or she is guilty or not guilty. It would have been very embarrassing for Bob to admit he did not know the meaning of the word. He told the judge that he needed to examine his papers to find the answer.

Bob was **stalling** until he could figure out what to say. As he looked through the papers, his good friend F. J. Lamb took a seat

WHI IMAGE ID 34808

next to him. Bob whispered to him, "For heaven's sake, tell me what it means to 'arraign' a prisoner!" Lamb, a lawyer with years of experience, told Bob what to say and saved him from being embarrassed. Despite this shaky beginning, Bob became a successful and popular district attorney.

This Dane County Courthouse was built in 1883 while Bob was district attorney. It was later torn down.

arraigned (uh **raynd**): to ask someone accused of a crime whether he or she is guilty or not guilty
stalling: delaying or pausing in order to have more time

As Bob was learning how to be district attorney, Belle's interest in law became helpful to her husband. Belle became a trusted adviser and counselor to her husband. When the need arose, she helped Bob with legal research and sometimes wrote **briefs** for him. One time when Bob was overwhelmed with work, he asked Belle to write a brief for an important case coming up before the **Supreme Court** of Wisconsin. After Bob's law firm won the case, **Chief Justice** Lyon remarked to Bob that his brief was "one of the best briefs **submitted** to the court in years." Bob proudly admitted, "That brief was written by Mrs. La Follette, an unknown but very able member of our **bar**—altogether the brainiest member of the family."

Belle performed a unique role in her marriage to Bob, whose rise to politics had only just begun. Later, when Bob ran for Congress, a reporter would comment that they worked together like a team. The reporter called the team "La Follette and La Follette."

brief: a paper that lists all the important facts about a court case **supreme court**: the highest court of law in a state or nation, made up of several judges **chief justice**: the highest judge in the supreme court **submitted**: handed in   **bar**: the group of lawyers allowed to practice law in a particular state

6

Even His Enemies Liked Him

While Bob was district attorney, he found a trusted friend and **mentor** in Judge George E. Bryant. Judge Bryant had a lot of experience in the courtroom, and he knew more about the law than Bob did. He also knew that Bob showed great promise as a leader. Judge Bryant encouraged his young friend to run for United States **Congress** in the 1884 election. Bob was young, but he was also determined. He followed Judge Bryant's advice and won the election in November of 1884. At just 29 years old, he became the youngest **state representative** in Congress! This election marked the beginning of 30 years of political offices Bob would hold as a congressman, governor, and senator.

In January of 1885, Bob and Belle moved to Washington, D.C., so that Bob could start his new job as a state representative for Wisconsin. This was the first time either Bob or Belle

mentor: a wise and trusted counselor or teacher   **Congress**: **cong** gris   **state representative**: one of several people chosen to speak and act for the people of a state

had traveled to the eastern part of the United States. They arrived in Washington early so that Bob could watch other congressmen in action and be prepared when his **term** in Congress began.

Two Houses of Congress

In the United States, we elect representatives to speak for our political beliefs in Congress. Congress is the part of our government where laws are made. It is made up of 2 "houses," the **Senate** and the House of Representatives. Each state elects 2 senators, but depending on how big or small its **population** is, it can elect many representatives. In 1884, Bob La Follette was elected by Wisconsin voters to the House of Representatives. His job was to represent the people of Wisconsin in the country's capital in Washington, D.C. He and Belle moved back and forth between Washington, D.C., and Madison during his years in Congress.

During their first few months in Washington, while Bob was in Congress, Belle spent much of her time in the **spectator's gallery**, listening with great interest to the discussion below. Often she took notes and then shared

term: in politics, the period of time one serves in an elected office   **Senate: sen** it   **population**: the total number of people living in a certain place   **spectator's gallery** (**spec** tay torz **gal** uh ree): the balcony where an audience can watch representatives discuss laws

Belle and Bob La Follette in 1885, the year Bob became a congressman and Belle became the first woman to graduate from the UW Law School.

ideas with Bob that she thought would be helpful in his work. Though many people gave Bob advice, Bob considered Belle his wisest and most trusted adviser. He appreciated her advice and called her "the ablest individual in the land."

Belle had many different roles in helping Bob. Part of her role was **practical**. She spent a great deal of time addressing and stuffing envelopes, writing letters, and keeping track of campaign posters. She also was Bob's chief political manager.

practical: useful in getting a task done

41

This meant she was in charge of his election **campaigns**. This was an important job, because in Congress, representatives are elected every 2 years. This meant that whenever Bob was not in Washington, he was busy working to win the next election.

During Bob's campaigns, Belle wrote speeches for him and helped plan **strategies** to win the election. When Bob was campaigning, Belle and Bob made a list of key **supporters** and sent Bob's most important speeches to them through the mail. These speeches kept them up to date and interested in Bob's work. When Belle mailed the speeches, she often included a free packet of seeds. She knew this personal touch would create goodwill among the farmers back home in Wisconsin.

Bob also asked Belle to make sure that his campaign speeches didn't last so long that his audience would get bored. Many times when Belle thought Bob had been talking for too long, she would signal him to stop. Sometimes he'd continue his speech, saying, "There's my wife shaking her

campaign: a period of time before an election when candidates try to get voters to vote for them
strategy: a clever plan to achieve a goal   **supporter**: in politics, one who gives money to a candidate to help with a campaign

Bob speaking to an excited crowd in Cumberland, Wisconsin, in 1897.

head and **looking daggers** at me. She thinks I'm talking too long." The crowd would laugh and urge him on. One farmer later recalled, "Why, he talked so long every darn cow in this part of the country was **bellerin'** to be milked but the crowd just kept **hollerin'** for Bob to go on."

looking daggers: to glare at angrily   **bellerin'**: slang for bellowing, to shout or yell   **hollerin'**: slang for hollering, yelling loudly

43

Belle didn't only help Bob with his campaigns. She also helped him think through what he stood for as a politician. She refused to support her husband without question. She was not afraid to let him know when she disagreed with his ideas. This forced Bob to think through his **positions** and often caused him to change his way of thinking. Belle set high standards and goals for Bob and demanded that he achieve them. When he won her hard-earned approval, Bob was convinced he had been right.

Winning elections turned out to be something the La Follettes were good at. Bob was re-elected to Congress in 1886 and 1888. He gained a reputation of being hard working and friendly. He was so well liked by his fellow representatives that one newspaper reported, "He is so good a fellow even his enemies like him."

position: in politics, a stance or view on a particular issue

No Free Ride for Bob

At the time of Bob's election to Congress, it was common for railroad companies to give politicians free tickets to ride the train. When Bob received his tickets, he gave them to his friend Sam Harper to keep in a sealed envelope, and he paid his own **fare**. Bob knew that he would be involved in making laws that affected railroads. He didn't want to owe any favors to the railroad companies or to accept gifts that might appear to be **bribes**. Bob chose to be honest, just like when he was a boy and refused to keep the pocketbook he found in the road. During the next 40 years of Bob's career in politics, he would become well known and respected for his honesty.

A train on Wisconsin's Central Locomotive line.

Bob refused to take free passes like this one given out in 1878.

---

fare: money paid to ride a train **bribe**: money or gifts offered illegally to someone to persuade him or her to do something for you

In 1890, despite his and Belle's hard work, Bob lost the re-election to the U.S. Congress. It was a terrible blow, but it wasn't unexpected. Bob was a member of the **Republican Party**, and that year, most of the people elected to Congress were members of the **Democratic Party**. Bob was defeated by a Democrat named Allen Bushnell. Although he was bitterly disappointed by the loss, Bob kept his sense of humor. After Bob learned that he'd lost the election, Belle **recalled**, "I couldn't believe when he came home at eleven o'clock and called upstairs in a matter-of-fact way, 'Well, Belle, Bushnell is elected to Congress, and I am elected to practice law.'"

Republican: ri **puhb** li kin   **Democratic**: dem uh **kra** tik   **Republican Party and Democratic Party**: the 2 major American political parties, both now and in the past   **recalled**: remembered

46

7

Fighting Bob

In 1891, after Bob lost the re-election to Congress, the La Follettes returned to Madison. Bob went back to being a lawyer and started arguing cases in court. He was so popular that when a big case came up, people lined up at the courthouse door hoping to get inside and see him in person.

Losing the election didn't mean Bob was finished with politics. Six months after he returned to Madison, something happened that paved the way for his next political campaign: running for **governor** of Wisconsin. Bob decided to become governor after he saw with his own eyes how dishonest politics had become in Wisconsin. In the spring of 1891, Bob was offered a bribe. **Philetus** Sawyer, a senator from Wisconsin, was one of the Republican leaders in the state. Senator Sawyer offered Bob money to **influence** a court case.

governor (**guhv** uh nur): the person elected as the head of the state to represent all the people in the state
Philetus: fI **lee** tis   **influence** (**in** floo ens): to get someone to do something or to think in a certain way

47

Senator Sawyer knew he would lose a lot of money if the case were lost. He wanted Bob to talk the judge into helping his side win the case so that he could keep the money. Later, he said didn't know that the judge for the case was Bob's brother-in-law, Robert Siebecker. Bob was furious that Sawyer would try to use money to control the court's decision. He refused to take the bribe, saying, "Senator Sawyer, you can't know what you are saying to me. If you struck me in the face you could not **insult** me as you insult me now."

This is Senator Philetus Sawyer, the man Bob battled over an illegal bribe.

Bob had always been known for his honesty. After refusing Senator Sawyer's bribe, he wanted to see that the rest of the government became more honest, too. For the next 10 years, Bob traveled around the state, speaking out against dishonest politicians and the **corruption** in Wisconsin's government. Eventually, Bob's campaign to "clean up" Wisconsin politics

insult: to offend or hurt with words   **corruption** (kuh **ruhp** shun): lack of honesty; willingness to accept bribes

led him to run for governor of Wisconsin. The governor is the most powerful lawmaker in the state. Bob knew that being governor would allow him to make the changes he thought were needed. Becoming governor wasn't easy, though. Bob had to run 3 times for governor before he was elected in 1900.

Bob's supporters wore campaign buttons to show they would vote for him.

What was Belle doing during this time? She was still giving Bob advice and helping him with his work. But she and Bob were also busy building a family. Their daughter Fola was already a teenager when her younger brothers and sister were born: Robert Jr. in 1895, Philip in 1897, and Mary in 1899. The family lived together in a big house near Madison's capitol building.

What Are Primary Elections?

Before Bob La Follette became a famous politician, people who ran for political office were not chosen to be candidates by a "popular" vote—that is, a vote by everyday citizens. Instead, they were **nominated** by a small group of men during a special **convention**. Only a few people were involved in selecting the names that would appear on the ballot. That means only a powerful and wealthy group of men could decide who would run for governor, senator, or congressman.

Bob La Follette believed that he was the "popular" choice for governor in 1896 and 1898—that is, he believed that if the people voted, he would be their first choice. But powerful men didn't want his name on the ballot. When the Republican convention was held, they made sure Bob was not nominated.

In 1900, Bob was finally elected as governor of Wisconsin. He wanted to change the unfair way candidates were chosen. America is a **democracy**, which means people choose their leaders. Bob felt that the citizens needed a more democratic way to choose their candidates. In 1905, Wisconsin passed a primary election law. The law allowed the people to choose which candidate the party would nominate for the general election. Later, the United States made this a law for presidential elections.

nominated (**nah** mi nay tud): chosen to run in an election   **convention**: a large gathering of people from the same political party   **democracy** (de **mok** ruh see): a system of government that allows people to choose their own candidates

During the 1900 campaign, Bob toured Wisconsin on a special campaign train. He gave 208 speeches in 61 counties in Wisconsin. Sometimes he'd make 10 to 15 speeches a day, 6 days a week! "It was dramatic and **excited** great interest," Bob wrote. Farmers would stop working and leave their farms to hear him speak. Factories, mines, and schools often closed when Bob came to town so that people would be free to attend his speeches.

Bob made speeches from a train car during the 1900 election for governor.

In 1900, Bob won the election for governor by more than 60,000 votes. He was a well-liked governor, and after his first term, he was re-elected twice, in 1902 and 1904. As governor, he worked tirelessly to keep his promise to make Wisconsin free of corruption.

excited: brought about, sparked

He also became a **reformer**. Like many reformers in the United States, Bob believed that the government had a responsibility to take care of its people, especially the poor and those with few rights.

Inside the Wisconsin Assembly Chamber, Governor Bob met with lawmakers to talk about new laws.

reformer: someone who wants to change things for the better

During his time as governor, Bob worked to pass laws in the state **legislature**. The legislature, like the Senate, met in the state capital in Madison to decide which laws would be passed for the state of Wisconsin.

Thanks to Bob, workers like these at Milwaukee's Meiselbach Bicycle Factory were the first in the country to have their rights protected by laws.

Although these laws were true only for Wisconsin, they were important because they became an example to the country as a whole.

Because of his fight against corruption and his work to help the powerless, Bob earned a nickname. Today, many people still call him by this name: "Fighting Bob."

legislature (**lej** uhs lay chur): an elected group of people who have the power to make or change laws for a state or nation

Lawmaker Bob

Helping those in need wasn't something Bob simply talked about. Here are some of the laws Bob helped pass.

Child Labor Laws

In 1900, when Bob became governor, many families sent their children to work in factories. Mothers and fathers could not earn enough money to take care of them. Some wanted their children to learn a **trade** like glassblowing. Factory owners often hired

Newsboys from Milwaukee in the early 1900s.

COURTESY OF THE MILWAUKEE COUNTY HISTORICAL SOCIETY

trade: a job that requires working with the hands or with machines

young workers because they did not have to pay them as much as they would a grown-up. In 1903, Wisconsin passed a law that required all child workers to be at least 14 years old. Children between 14 and 16 had to have a **work permit**. In 1907, Bob helped the Wisconsin legislature pass **child labor** laws that kept children from working dangerous jobs, like operating machines or climbing on high ladders. Wisconsin was one of the first states to pass laws that protected young workers.

Workers' Rights

Men, women, and children who worked in Wisconsin's factories were often forced to work in unhealthy buildings with dangerous equipment. In Milwaukee in 1900, many factories had poor lighting, heating, and **ventilation**. Workers were forced to breathe harmful or poisonous air. Machines often were unsafe. Accidents were common, and workers hurt on the job were unlikely to receive **compensation**.

Bob led the fight in Wisconsin to protect workers' rights. He helped pass a law that made employers pay for medical care when an employee got hurt at work and made them provide money while the worker had to stay home from the job. It was the first law of its kind to be passed in the United States!

work permit: a piece of paper signed by an official that gives someone permission to work   **child labor**: the use of children as workers in factories, farms, and mines   **ventilation**: system that allows fresh air into a room and sends stale air out   **compensation**: money a worker gets when he or she is hurt on the job

8

We Can't Have the Governor's Son Sucking His Thumb

What was it like growing up as the children of Belle and Bob La Follette? By the time Phil, their second son, was 10 years old, his father was a senator. Before that, he had

been governor. He had been a famous politician for as long a Phil could remember. As a very young child, Phil remembered his grandmother coming into his room. He was looking at a picture book and sucking his thumb. His grandmother said to

Bobbie and Phil playing horse on the lawn of the Governor's Mansion.

him, "Phil, your father has just been elected governor of Wisconsin, and we can't have the governor's son sucking his thumb."

Phil had a brother, Robert or "Bobbie," who was 2 years older than he was, and a sister, Mary, who was 2 years younger. He also had an older sister, Fola, who was already 15 by the time he was

Belle with Bobbie and Phil in a picture taken for Bob Sr. for Christmas in 1904.

born. All of the children grew up surrounded by politics. In some ways, this made their childhoods very different from those of other kids, and in other ways, their childhoods were much the same as other kids.

Phil, Mary, and Bobbie play cops and robbers at Maple Bluff Farm.

Bob La Follette takes a break with his family. Belle is seated, left, with Mary and a family friend on the porch.

Bobbie, Phil, and Mary loved to dress up and play make-believe. Mary later recalled, "When Phil and I played together, which we did a lot . . . we would dress up in fancy clothes. Phil would be the king or **Napoleon**. I would be the princess; Bobbie wouldn't **deign** to play in these games. He particularly liked to tease Phil. I would always come to Phil's defense."

Another time, the children were playing "detective" after having just read a detective story.

Napoleon (nuh **poh** lee uhn): a famous general who became the ruler of France at the end of the 1790s
deign (dayn): to lower oneself

58

Mary was the robber, Phil the detective, and Bobbie the judge. Belle wrote a letter to their father in Washington as they played. She joked, "Well, dear, there is so much shooting and dying about me that I think I shall have to stop writing for a while and give the house over to the **distinguished** assassins and their victims."

When Bob was the governor of Wisconsin, his family lived in the governor's mansion near the state capitol in a neighborhood called "Big Bug Hill." The kids sometimes got into mischief. One afternoon, Belle noticed that many of the visitors to the

Phil on horseback in front of Governor's Mansion in 1904.

mansion were smiling after they'd passed through the front door.

distinguished (dis **ting** guishd): well known and respected

When Belle went to investigate, she saw Bobbie sitting on a chair with his feet up on a railing on the front porch. He was holding a piece of string attached to the screen door. As guests approached, he'd open the door by pulling on the string. Belle laughed.

Another time, Bobbie and Phil discovered a hidden **register** under a rug in their bedroom. It was located right over the dining room. The 2 boys decided to spy on their parents

WHI IMAGE ID 30467

Like father, like son. Bob Sr. and Bob Jr. share a book in their Washington, D.C., home.

and their guests during a "very special dinner." Phil recalled, "Everything was going splendidly at the dinner. We rolled up the rug and carefully opened the register and

register: a vent for heating

60

looked down into the dining room. To our horror a large black spot appeared right in the middle of a white tablecloth. The **accumulated** dust and dirt of a decade had been dumped on the table. Bobbie and I thought we were surely in for it now. We were wrong. Mother and Father treated it as a joke and we went **scot-free** for that one."

It wasn't always easy to be the son or daughter of a famous politician. Many of the women who lived in their neighborhood ignored the governor and his wife because they disagreed with Bob's politics. However, they also were curious about social events at the mansion and sometimes tried to get information from the La Follette children. Phil remembered, "I was asked how Mother arranged the seating of the guests at formal dinners. Of course I knew the answer: 'She seats first a **dull** person and then a bright person, and so on around the table.' That one went around town in a hurry. And **thereafter**, guests at our table would good-naturedly wonder who was who."

accumulated (uh **kyoom** yoo lay tud): gathered, piled up   **scot-free**: without being punished   **dull**: boring
thereafter: after that

After Bob became a senator in 1905, the children spent some of their time in Washington, D.C., but most of the time they lived in Madison with their grandparents. In the fall of 1905, Bob and Belle rode horseback over the countryside around Madison looking for a farm, something they had wanted since before they were married. The couple finally chose a 60-acre farm in Maple Bluff, 3.5 miles from Madison. Their farm was right on the shores of Lake Mendota.

The Maple Bluff farm had a herd of dairy cows, 11 acres of plum and cherry trees, and many **Shetland ponies**. Bob and Belle loved horses, and the children learned to ride when they were very young. Phil started to ride when he was only 3 years old.

Mary and Phil La Follette taking care of the ponies at Maple Bluff Farm.

Shetland ponies: a breed of ponies from the Shetland islands off the coast of Scotland, known for their small size

Bobbie, Phil, and Mary all cared for the ponies. They fed and watered them, brushed them daily, and cleaned out their stalls. In return, the children were allowed to ride and train the ponies and drive them hitched to a cart. Often during the summer and fall, the children would load the cart with boxes of fresh vegetables or fruit and drive a few miles into town to sell their produce. Sometimes Bobbie and Phil knocked on people's back doors to sell cherries. The senator's children and their ponies soon became a familiar sight on the streets of Madison.

Occasionally, the children even raced their ponies. As Phil later wrote, "The big event of the year for me was the county fair. One year it was decided to have a pony race. I was in the lead as we came down the home stretch, when suddenly something frightened Jessie, my horse, and she stopped **abruptly**. I jumped off, grabbed her bridle and led her over the finish line. The rules were not strict and I was declared the winner."

abruptly (uh **brup** lee): suddenly

63

Being the children of political leaders also meant that they received a "political education" at home. When Phil was 11 and Bobbie was 13, Bob encouraged them to attend many of his meetings. Many of these meetings were held in the study at home. Bobbie and Phil often sat silently, listening to the adults

WHI IMAGE ID 27038

as they talked about politics and discussed strategies to reach their goals.

Belle recalled an incident that showed how closely Bobbie and Phil paid attention during political discussions. On March 17, 1908, Belle was in the

The La Follette family in 1917. Bob Sr., Mary, Belle, and Phil are seated, and Bob Jr. is standing.

spectator's gallery of the U.S. Senate with several close friends and 13-year-old Bobbie. They were listening to a discussion about a **bill** that Bob did not agree with. Bob was at home working on a speech that argued against the bill. During the discussion, Senator Nelson Aldrich of **Rhode** Island suggested some changes to the bill that would make Bob's speech much less powerful. Belle turned to ask Bobbie if she had heard the senator correctly. She later wrote, "I noticed that Bob Jr. had left the gallery. He was soon back again. 'I got Daddy on the telephone before he had left the house and told him what happened,' he whispered." The quick wit of his 13-year-old son, who had rushed out to warn his father about Aldrich's announcement, gave Bob enough time to change his speech to respond to Senator Aldrich.

Bob and Belle had high **expectations** for their children. Throughout their lives, the children worried that they would fail to measure up to those expectations. Phil wrote to his father, "I know that it will take an almost **superhuman** effort on any of our parts to even **approximate** living up to you." But approximate their father they did.

bill: a plan for a new law   **Rhode** (rohd)   **expectations**: hopes   **superhuman**: beyond ordinary human ability
approximate (uh **prok** si mayt): to come close to

65

Both Phil and Bobbie went on to have successful political careers. Fola became a spokeswoman for women's rights, and Mary married a lawyer who helped with Bob's campaigns.

Like his father, Bob Jr. became a famous senator.

Phil grew up to become governor of Wisconsin and was elected 3 times in the 1930s.

When They Grew Up

What happened to the La Follette children when they grew up? All 4 worked for a time in Bob's senate office. Fola, the oldest, became an actress in New York City. Like her mother, she made speeches arguing for women's right to vote. She also spent 22 years finishing the biography of her father that Belle had begun. It was published in 1953 and was 1,305 pages long! Bob Jr. took his father's place as a Wisconsin senator in 1925. He served as the United States senator from Wisconsin until 1946—more than 20 years. Phil, like his father, was a great public speaker. He became a lawyer and served as district attorney in Madison, and later as the governor of Wisconsin. He was governor 3 times in the 1930s. Phil and Bob Jr. were also leaders in Wisconsin's Progressive Party. Mary, the youngest of the La Follette kids, devoted her energies to painting and to raising her children.

Like grandfather, like grandson. Bob Jr.'s son Bronson—Fighting Bob's grandson—became the attorney general of Wisconsin and ran for governor of Wisconsin in 1968. When you grow up, do you think you'll do the same kind of work that your parents or grandparents did?

9

Mrs. La Follette Can Run!

While Bob was practicing law in Madison during the 1890s, Belle became interested in physical exercise and **nutrition**. In the 1800s, wealthy women had been told they should not do hard work or pursue higher education. People thought that too much physical or mental effort would harm women's fragile bodies and threaten the health of the children they might have. **Proper** women did not exercise, and they did not usually go to college.

Belle already had rebelled against **tradition** by going to college and to law school. She also rebelled by wearing comfortable, loose-fitting clothing rather than **corsets** and heavy skirts. She did this years before it was common for women to dress more casually. Many years later, she'd speak against practices such as the wearing of corsets. Getting young

nutrition: the science of healthy eating **proper**: strictly following rules, especially in behavior **tradition**: a way of life passed down from generation to generation **corset**: a close-fitting undergarment worn to support and shape the waistline, hips, and breasts

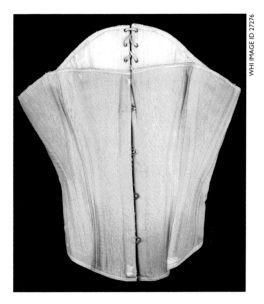

In 1900, "proper" women wore stiff corsets, like the one on the right, under their dresses to give them slim waists and good posture.

women out of their tight corsets and bulky layers of skirts was a major step in freeing them.

In 1893, Belle asked Emily Bishop, the principal of a **fitness school** in New York, to visit Madison. Fitness schools were popular in the late 1800s. Long before going to the gym became a popular way to keep fit, these schools encouraged women to be physically active. When Bishop came, she spoke at Ladies Hall, the dormitory where Belle had lived during her college days. Many women attended that meeting.

fitness school: a school for exercise, popular in the late 1800s

Bishop believed that exercise and practicing deep breathing strengthened the mind. She created a set of exercises women could do while saying phrases such as "slower, deeper breathing means calmer, healthier thought" and "strengthen the **diaphragm** and you strengthen the will." Along with exercise, she encouraged women to eat fresh vegetables, **citrus** fruit, eggs, lean meat, and skim milk. Sugar and fat were completely avoided.

What Belle liked most about Emily Bishop's program was the idea that if women were mentally and physically fit, they

WHI IMAGE ID 4008

would be able to build a better world. Many of the women in Madison also liked Bishop's ideas. So many women were interested that they decided to organize their own fitness school. Belle became the school's president and remained so for the next 10 years.

Girls playing outdoor basketball in 1900.

diaphragm (dl uh fram): the wall of muscle between the chest and the stomach   **citrus**: orange, lime, or lemon

70

Belle directed the fitness program and exercised regularly
with other Madison women. At the school she taught women
to breathe deeply, to sweat without feeling guilty, to stretch
their muscles, and to discover their physical capabilities. For
the rest of her life, she encouraged women to exercise and
eat well.

Women exercising in a physical education class in 1911.

Belle also wrote about exercise and health. In 1909, Belle and Bob started their own magazine, *La Follette's Weekly Magazine*. Belle was the **editor** of the "Home and Education" section. She wrote weekly and later monthly **columns** in the magazine for the next 20 years. Belle began writing articles that encouraged healthy eating, nutrition, fresh air, and exercise. Her first column dealt with the most **trivial** health subject you could imagine: yawning.

WHI IMAGE ID 30384

Belle La Follette in 1905.

"The only way to strengthen the body is by use. Stretch and yawn," she told women readers, "a great big natural yawn. Stretch as a cat stretches, gradually energize the whole body, stretching from the top of the head to the tip of the toes and at the same time opening the mouth wide, **drawing** a great big long breath, filling the lungs full, getting a splendid sense of freedom; then relax and feel the perfect rest of letting go."

editor: a person who decides what should go in a magazine or book   **column** (**kah** luhm): an article by the same person that appears regularly in a newspaper or magazine   **trivial**: unimportant   **drawing**: breathing in

The Truth Shall Make You Free

Since the time Bob owned and edited the *University Press* in college, he was eager to create his own magazine. Nearly 30 years after graduating from the University of Wisconsin, he achieved his dream. On January 9, 1909, Bob and Belle started *La Follette's Weekly Magazine* to make their **progressive** ideas better known. The magazine's cover showed a hand holding a pen, writing, "The Truth" with the **motto** above it, "Ye shall know the truth and the truth shall make you free."

Bob and Belle started La Follette's Weekly Magazine in 1909.

In 1929, *La Follette's Weekly Magazine* changed its name to *The Progressive*, in part because their political views had grown into an entire political party of "Progressives." *The Progressive* still exists today. Its goal is to be a voice for peace, equality, and a healthy environment. For nearly 100 years, *The Progressive* has taken stands on the important political and **ethical** issues of the day. Do you agree with the issues Belle and Bob La Follette thought were most important?

progressive (proh **gres** iv): in favor of reform or improvement   **motto**: a short sentence that states what someone believes in or stands for   **ethical**: having to do with what is good and bad, and how people treat one another in groups

In later columns, she wrote about running or fast walking as a cure for **depression**. "There is no such good all-around exercise as running. Running gives a delightful sense of lightness and youth to the body. Unfortunately it is not considered proper for women to run and there are few places where one can run without the depressing fear of being seen. The standing run is a good substitute. Stand **before** a mirror—we should use mirrors more for this purpose—take the running step over and over. Let the arms hang relaxed. Run at least 100 steps as a daily exercise. It will lighten the step and brighten the mind."

Belle ran regularly for many years. After the La Follettes moved into their Maple Bluff farm, Belle jogged a mile or 2 every morning on the privacy of their own land. She often led her children in exercises. As part of her campaign to keep her family healthy, Belle also baked her own whole-grain breads and cakes and prepared low-fat, nutritious meals with vegetables from the garden.

depression (dee **pre** shun): a state of long-lasting unhappiness   **before**: in front of

Newspapers sometimes commented on Belle's commitment to exercise and health. In 1904, under the headline, "Mrs. La Follette Can Run," a Detroit newspaper reported: "The wife of the governor of Wisconsin is said to be an enthusiastic **dress** reformer and **builds** much also on physical exercise of all sorts. She is said to get up early and take a 2-mile run before breakfast."

dress: clothing   **builds**: believes in

10

The Best Orator in America

By the time he became governor in 1900, Bob had proved that he was a great public speaker. He had given speeches in front of an audience from the time he was a child in school all the way through college. He used his speaking skills in the courtroom as a lawyer and on the campaign trail as a politician.

When Bob become governor he didn't give up public speaking. He traveled around the country giving speeches on **Chautauqua** speaking tours. Each summer in many towns throughout the United States, a large tent with a platform and folding chairs would hold audiences of 1,500 to 2,000 people. Bob often spoke to **spellbound** audiences for 3 hours straight. He would leave the stage dripping with sweat. In Bob's presentations, he'd act out parts from William Shakespeare's play *Hamlet* or give speeches describing ways to improve

Chautauqua (chuh **tawk** wah): a traveling education show with lectures, plays, and musical performances popular in the early 1900s   **spellbound**: on the edge of their seats

the government. In his speeches, he spread the message of Progressive politics far and wide.

WHI IMAGE ID 32540

Bob giving a speech in front of large crowd in Decator, Illinois, in 1905.

Travel between the towns where he spoke was hard because trains were frequently late. Sometimes he could not get good food and would become ill because of the poor diet or water. He'd often feel lonely and guilty about being separated from his family, but he knew he needed to earn the money. In spite of these difficulties, he found strength and **inspiration** in the excitement of his audience.

inspiration (ins puh **ray** shun): something that encourages and influences someone to do something

"The Most American Thing in America"

The Chautauqua movement was founded in 1874 in the town of Chautauqua, New York. The original idea was to educate teachers from small towns, but Chautauqua soon became a place where families could gather in the summertime for several days of learning and enjoyment. People came from miles around to a camp along the shore of Lake Chautauqua. There, they heard speakers, listened to bands, enjoyed plays, dined together. They talked about politics, books, music, and science.

Around 1900, traveling Chautauquas were introduced across the country. The traveling Chautauquas held programs in public halls and in huge, circus-like tents. Eventually, permanent Chautauqua parks were built. They included auditoriums, dining halls, arts and crafts centers, classrooms, and even cottages for visitors to stay in. The Chautauqua performers were teachers, preachers, explorers, scientists, politicians, musicians, **glee clubs**, jugglers, magicians, and even whistlers and yodelers.

glee club: a chorus of singers

When the Chautauqua came to town, it provided entertainment for the whole family and the entire community. Theodore Roosevelt, who was president during the time Bob La Follette was a senator, was so impressed by Chautauqua that he called it "the most American thing in America."

The Chautauqua movement ended around 1924, when radio shows and movies became more popular forms of entertainment. Would you rather attend a live performance or watch TV? Why?

A Chautauqua meeting in Racine, Wisconsin.

Because of his reforms and his strong leadership, Bob proved to be a popular governor. But he wanted to make even more of a difference. In 1905, Bob ran for United States Senate and won. As a senator, he would be able to create laws that would affect the entire nation, not just Wisconsin. In 1906, Bob quit his job as governor and became one of 2 senators from the state of Wisconsin. He and Belle prepared to move back to Washington, D.C.

WHI IMAGE ID 10650

"Fighting Bob" La Follette in 1906.

When Bob took his Senate seat in January 1906, it already was known throughout the nation that he was a first-rate speaker and successful reformer. But he was not welcomed when he arrived in the Senate. Even though he was well known beyond Wisconsin, there was an **unwritten rule** in the Senate that new senators should be "seen but not heard." The other senators made it clear that they expected Bob to be **humble** and silent. Instead, Bob immediately made a major speech. Many senators left the Senate floor to show they did not like Bob speaking when he should be silent. Rather than apologizing, Bob warned them that they might have to leave the Senate if they didn't change *their* behavior.

For the next 20 years, Bob continued to be a forceful speaker on the Senate floor. He fought for the same kinds of reforms he had won in Wisconsin. He held tightly to the causes he believed in, even when they were unpopular or angered his fellow senators. Eventually, his stubbornness earned him great respect.

unwritten rule: a rule that is followed but not written down   **humble**: not proud

It's Roll Call Time!

How did Bob get so many politicians to vote for his laws? Just as a teacher calls attendance in class, Bob used a "roll call" for the politicians who helped to make laws in Wisconsin. During his campaign for governor in 1904, Bob traveled to the hometowns of congressmen and senators around Wisconsin. When he was convinced they had not voted as they had promised, he'd tell the crowd how they actually had voted. This reading of the roll call changed how people decided who to vote for.

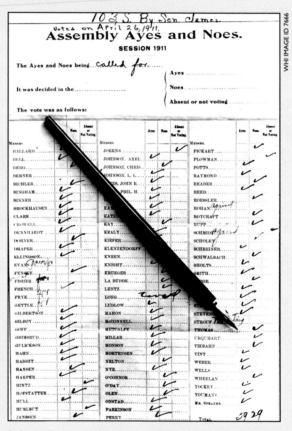

Bob used records like this to tell how senators had voted when he read his "roll call." The ayes meant yes, and the noes meant no.

Instead of judging politicians by their personality, Bob's roll call introduced the idea that voters should judge politicians by whether or not they kept their promises. Their votes, after all, were supposed to represent the people who voted for them.

Bob would continue to read the roll call when he became a United States Senator. Before long, other politicians began to use this same strategy. The reading of the roll call would eventually change the way politicians ran their campaigns throughout the entire country. They made politics more honest because they ensured that politicians had to keep to their word.

Just as when he was Wisconsin's governor, many of the changes Bob wanted to make had to do with the rights of women, children, and others with few rights. He was also concerned with workers' rights. Bob won his first battle in the Senate in January 1907 by reading the "roll call." In the spring of 1906, Bob had introduced a bill to limit the number of hours railroad companies could ask their employees to work in a row.

At that time, railroad workers sometimes had to work 24 or even 36 hours without stopping! Accidents sometimes occurred because the workers were so tired. Bob wanted railroad workers to work fewer hours back-to-back. The *New York Times* reported that La Follette's reading of the roll call was the reason the bill became a law. After Bob read the roll call, more senators were willing to vote for the rights of railway

WHI IMAGE ID 24801

As a senator, Bob fought for the rights of railway workers.

workers. This was because they didn't want to be known as men who were cruel or who accepted bribes from the railroads. The Senate passed Bob's hours-of-service bill by a roll-call vote of 70 to 1.

Just as Bob helped to protect railroad workers, he also was responsible for a law that protected sailors and passengers on ships. Before the La Follette Seamen's Act became a law, sailors had very few rights. They weren't allowed to leave a ship after the **cargo** was unloaded, even though they had been on the sea for weeks or months. Bob's bill allowed sailors to leave ships after the cargo was unloaded rather than having to work on the ship for an entire year. The bill had other features that ensured the safety of the sailors. Ships had to carry enough lifeboats and rafts for all passengers and crew members. They were also required to have 2 experienced seamen for each lifeboat, and to practice what they would do in an emergency. Just a few years earlier, in 1912, the *Titanic* had sunk. The ship did not have enough lifeboats, and 1,600 passengers lost their lives in the icy water. This tragic event helped to get Bob's bill passed in 1915.

Bob helped to pass many other laws while he was a senator. He supported a law that made all United States workers pay taxes on the money they earned. He also promoted laws that conserved natural resources and public land, so that the wood on these lands would be protected. And as always, he encouraged honesty in the government.

cargo: goods that are carried by ship or airplane

11

Are Women Not People, Too?

Belle worked tirelessly helping Bob because she truly believed in his causes. She shared in every aspect of his work. She also fought for many causes of her own. This was especially true in her fight for women's rights and for **racial equality**. Belle's belief that women are valuable members of society can be traced back to her family. As a child, she greatly admired her grandmother for her determination and hard work, and her mother for the sacrifices she made so that Belle could attend college.

Belle fought hardest for women's right to vote, or **suffrage**. She believed that equality between men and women would mean better homes and a better government for everyone. She argued that society works best when men and women have equal rights and "share with each other the **solution** of their common problems." Belle believed equality was a

racial equality (**ray** shul ee **kwah** li tee): people of all races having the same rights   **suffrage** (**suhf** rij): the right to vote   **solution**: answer or remedy

question of fairness. If America was a democracy—that is, a government where everyone was allowed a say—then shouldn't women have the right to vote?

Belle fought for women's rights in several different ways. She organized **rallies** and marched in parades. She used her legal knowledge to **lobby** for the

These women wore **bloomers** to show their support for the suffrage movement.

health and education of women and children. Belle even used her columns in *La Follette's Weekly Magazine* to make the case for women's suffrage. She wrote "Women of the Hour," a special column in the magazine. In this column, she wrote about the achievements of **suffragettes**.

rally: a gathering of a large group of people for a specific cause   **bloomers**: loose pants gathered at the knee, worn by women suffragettes to show their independence   **lobby**: to try to influence someone to vote a certain way   **suffragette** (suf ruh **jet**): a woman who fought for the right to vote in the early 1900s

WHI IMAGE ID 1932

This poster tried to convince people that the women's vote was a **menace** or danger to society.

Just as Belle had stage fright in her college speech class, she was a **reluctant** speaker as an adult. In spite of this, Belle overcame her shyness and gave many speeches on women's rights. In 1914, she gave speeches on women's suffrage 64 days in a row! But Belle confessed to her daughter Mary that she never liked public speaking. She said,

"Even now after all my experience I suffer with anxiety and when I was your age, it was *agony* for me to even *recite* in class."

menace (**men** is): a threat or danger   reluctant: not wanting to do something

WHI IMAGE ID 2415

Though she was often nervous, Belle was a persuasive speaker for women's rights.

In 1913, Belle went to Washington, D.C., to speak to the Senate Committee on Women's Suffrage. In her speech, she repeated the words spoken by Abraham Lincoln in the Gettysburg Address: "This Nation shall have a new birth of freedom, and government of the people, by the people, for the people shall not **perish** from the Earth." Belle then added

perish: disappear, die

WHI IMAGE ID 5157

What message do these suffragettes hope to get across?

the question: "Are women not people, too?" The committee, which was made up of only men, broke into applause. Just as she had done in college, Belle was able to speak clearly and effectively to an audience.

It wasn't until 1919, however, that women were allowed to vote in America. Belle was visiting her daughter Mary when she first heard the news. She was thrilled. She looked at her daughter and realized that Mary now had the same right to vote as her brothers had on their twenty-first birthdays. Belle was as pleased for her daughter as she had been for her sons.

While fighting for the rights of women, Belle also fought for racial equality. In 1913, she took up the cause of 3 young black women who worked for the United States Treasury Department. One of these women had been fired from her

90

job because she sat down at a table assigned to white women employees. The woman was told she was fired for **disrespectful** behavior. At the time, black and white workers were not allowed to sit together. This was part of a government policy called **segregation** meant to keep people of different races apart. Belle complained about this unfair policy to President Wilson himself, but he refused to change the policy or to hire the woman again.

Belle was angry that she was unable to help the woman, so she wrote columns about this case in *La Follette's Weekly Magazine*. She criticized President Wilson for his policies and argued the woman should not have lost her job. Not all of her readers agreed with Belle. After the articles were published, many of her readers refused to buy the magazine, and some sent angry letters to her. Belle decided to print some of these letters in *La Follette's Weekly Magazine*. One letter threatened, "This does not raise you very much in the estimation of decent white people. Don't do it again." Unafraid, Belle continued to write columns arguing for equality, and she spoke out against racial segregation in her speeches.

disrespectful: lacking respect; rude   **segregation**: the practice of keeping groups apart based on the color of their skin

12

Even His Friends Called Him a Traitor

In the Senate, Bob fought hard for the causes he believed in and for the laws he thought should be passed. His ideas were not always popular, but this didn't stop Bob from standing firm. Sometimes his stubbornness got him into trouble.

By 1914, the most powerful countries in Europe had organized themselves into 2 **opposing** groups. Germany, Italy, and Austria-Hungary were on one side, and France, Great Britain, and Russia were on the other. When fighting broke out between the 2 sides, Bob became one of the leaders of a movement that wanted to keep the United States out of the war. His strong opinions led some people to consider him to be "the most hated man in America."

opposing: on opposite sides, disagreeing

Bob believed the war was being fought in Europe because the countries who were **involved** wanted power and influence. He believed their disagreements should be solved peacefully, without fighting. He said the United States should not be involved in the war and should not sell weapons to any of the countries involved in the fighting.

WHI IMAGE ID 3272

In this political cartoon, Bob La Follette is shown with the ruler of Germany who is pinning medals on him. Many people believed Bob took Germany's side in the war, but this was not true.

When President Wilson wanted the United States to **declare** war on Germany in 1917, only 6 senators voted against it. Bob was one of them.

involved: taking part in   **declare**: to announce something formally

The years between 1914 and 1918 were a difficult time for Wisconsin. Many Wisconsin residents felt great **loyalty** to the European country that was their home before they came to the United States. This was especially true for Wisconsin's large German American population. When the United States declared war on Germany on April 6, 1917, things changed. Most German Americans felt they needed to support the United States, not Germany.

Despite their loyalty to America, German Americans became a target for people's anger and violence. In 1917 and 1918, many people in Wisconsin treated anything German with **suspicion**. Some Wisconsin towns refused to teach the German language in their schools. German-language books were burned in Wisconsin streets. People with German names were attacked or treated as if they might be spies. During these dangerous times when loyalty and **patriotism** were constantly questioned, Bob led the fight against the United States entering war. His position angered many of Wisconsin's citizens who supported the war. They questioned whether he was loyal to the country.

loyalty: faithful to one's country, family, friends, or beliefs **suspicion**: mistrust, doubt **patriotism**: love for one's country

Bob had even more trouble after he gave a speech in St. Paul, Minnesota, on September 20, 1917. Two years earlier, Germany had sunk a British ship, the *Lusitania*, with torpedoes from a submarine. Many Americans had died in that disaster. After Bob's speech, newspapers reported that he had **defended** Germany's action. But the newspapers got the story wrong. They **misquoted** what Bob said. Bob said that the United States had a "**grievance** against Germany"—that is, a reason to be angry with Germany. The newspaper reported that he said the opposite, that the United States had "*no* grievance against Germany."

LIBRARY OF CONGRESS LC-USZ62-62966

Bob pounds his fist to make his point clear during a speech in Washington, D.C.

defended: supported, argued for   **misquoted**: incorrectly wrote down the words someone has said
grievance (**gree** vins): reason to be angry

When the article was printed, hatred against Bob exploded. People were furious with him. From coast to coast, people called him a **traitor** and "pro-German." Many of his good friends attacked him. Some senators wanted him to leave the Senate.

Eight months after his speech in St. Paul, the newspapers admitted that Bob had been misquoted and apologized to him. Almost a year and a half later, after the war ended, the Senate admitted it had been wrong about Bob. Bob was relieved by this, but he was angry and upset that he'd been attacked for something he'd never said.

Bob reads a letter at his desk.

traitor: someone who aids the enemy of his or her country

Give Peace a Chance

Just as Bob strongly opposed World War I, Belle fought for world peace. She wanted to see every nation in the world **disarm**, or lay down their weapons. She believed that using war to "settle differences among nations" was as useless as "**dueling** was in times past to settle differences among individuals."

In January 1915, Belle became one of the founders of the Woman's Peace Party (WPP). The goal of the WPP was to bring an end to World War I. Belle also protested against the military **draft**, which made it a rule for men to have to go to war even if they didn't sign up. She thought that the posters the military put up to encourage men to join the fighting were not honest. They made war seem like a fun adventure instead of something that was dangerous and serious.

Belle believed that women had a special role in promoting world peace. On December 23, 1920, after the war had ended, she led the "peace on earth" rally in Washington. Freezing temperatures did not prevent Belle from voicing her opinions. "We women have the power to **compel** disarmament," she said. "We need not **plead** or beg. We have the **ballot**. . . . We vow to use our votes to defeat those who stand for **militarism** and war; and to elect those who stand for peace and disarmament." Her efforts and those of thousands of women like her encouraged senators and representatives to pass a bill in 1922 that led to the first official meeting about disarming.

disarm: when a country gives up its weapons   dueling (doo ling): formal combat between 2 persons to the death   draft: a law that requires men to fight in war   compel: to make someone do something   plead: to ask with great emotion   ballot: the vote   militarism (mil i tur i zum): love of war

By 1922, 5 years had passed since Bob had taken his stand against the United States entering World War I. When he was running for Senate once again, he gave a speech in the state capitol building in Madison. He hadn't given a speech in Madison in 4 years. When the day of the speech arrived, the capitol was full of citizens eager to hear their senator speak. Bob began his speech by expressing his thanks to his friends and neighbors for welcoming him back to the place where he was born and had lived his entire life.

Bob speaking from the steps of the capitol building in Madison in November 1924.

"Then," his son Phil recalled, "he changed. The muscles of his jaw tightened. His blue eyes shot fire. He raised his right arm, fingers together, hand upright and waving **aloft** like a banner. 'I am going to be a candidate for re-election to the United States Senate. I do not want the vote of a single citizen under any **misapprehension** of where I stand: I would not change my **record** on the war for that of any man, living or dead.'"

There was stunned silence. In no uncertain terms, Bob had said that he would not take back his position on the war, even though the war was over. The crowd had expected Bob to apologize for taking a position that had angered so many people and caused him so many problems. Instead, he showed no **regret**. "Fightin'" Bob was still standing strong. Wave after wave of applause rang out. A member of the state senate who had fought against Bob for many years sat down with tears running down his cheeks. He said that he hated La Follette, "but my God, what guts he's got." Bob won his election to Senate that year by a record-breaking number of votes.

aloft: high up in the air   **misapprehension** (mis ap ree **hen** shun): not understanding   **record**: stand, stance
regret: being sorry for something that happened in the past

Two years later, Bob disagreed with the positions of both the Democratic and Republican Parties. So did many politicians and voters in Wisconsin and other states in the Midwest. Many farmers and labor union workers believed Bob had the power and vision to make change happen. With their support, Bob formed a new political party and put in his bid to run for president of the United States. He called his new party the **Progressive Party**. During his campaign, Bob made many promises. He promised to support farmers with easy ways to borrow money. He promised to make child labor illegal. And he promised to make it a law that the president couldn't declare war unless the people voted for it. Belle helped

Bob's supporters bought these certificates to help him raise money when he ran for president in 1924.

Progressive Party: political party formed by Bob La Follette and his followers in the early 1900s to make positive changes in government, education, and rights

on the campaign, too. In 1924, she was one of the first presidential candidate's wives to give campaign speeches.

Even though Bob had a strong **platform**, he didn't have a strong chance of winning. For one thing, the Progressive Party was brand new, but the

Bob campaigning at Yankee Stadium in New York in 1924. His son, Bob Jr., is behind the senator to the left.

Democratic and Republican Parties had been around for more than 100 years. For another, Bob's health was failing. Bob was now 69 years old, and he had been sick for a very long time. When his doctors told him that the campaign might kill him, Bob said to his son Phil, "I have had a wonderful life. I'd like to live it all over again. But I don't want to—I just can't—live rolled up in a cotton blanket. . . . I want to die, as

platform: a set of beliefs of a political party on the important issues of the day

101

I have lived, with my boots on." Until the very end, he vowed to keep fighting political battles.

Bob lost the 1924 election for president, but he received 4,822,319 votes—more votes than any **independent** candidate had ever received in a presidential election.

The La Follette family and friends listens to the results of the 1924 presidential election on the radio.

independent: not Republican or Democrat

13

The Progressive Torch Keeps Burning

Four days after his seventieth birthday on June 18, 1925, Bob died in his home in Washington, D.C., with his family gathered around his bedside. Everyone agreed he should be buried in his home state of Wisconsin. Hundreds of people lined the streets of Madison when Bob was laid to rest. The minister who led the funeral service said, "We say farewell, but we shall always remember him." A few days later, the *Chicago Tribune* carried the story of Bob's

WHI IMAGE ID 32420

At Bob La Follette's funeral.

burial in Madison with the headline, "Fighting Bob, on his Shield, Home at Last." In ancient Greece, brave warriors were expected to return home either "with" their shield, meaning alive and victorious, or "on" their shield, meaning they died as a hero in battle. The newspaper was saying that Bob had died as a hero.

The *Sheboygan Press* printed this cartoon after Bob died. How did the cartoonist feel about Bob?

Bob's death didn't mean that Belle was done with her political work. In fact, when Bob died, many voters and politicians from Wisconsin wanted Belle to take Bob's place in the Senate. This would have made her the first woman senator in the United States, but she decided against it. Instead, she told supporters that she wished to continue writing her columns and to work on her new project. She wanted to write a biography about Bob's life. Belle asked voters to

Bob Jr. and Phil walk with Belle down the capitol steps at Bob's funeral.

elect her son, Bobbie, to take his father's place in the Senate. The idea was a good one, and Bob Jr. was elected to the senate.

During the next 6 years, Belle worked on Bob's biography and served as an editor, writer, and **publisher** for *La Follette's Weekly Magazine*. As she had been with her husband, she also was her son's most trusted adviser during his years in the Senate.

publisher: the person in charge of a magazine

On August 16, 1931, at the age of 71, Belle went to the hospital for a regular checkup. The visit was supposed to take only an hour. During the exam, however, the doctor accidentally punctured her intestines. She died 2 days later. At her funeral, her friend Lincoln Steffens remembered a time at the Maple Bluff farm when Belle had ridden her horse so fast that he could barely keep up. "She wanted to fly," said Steffens. "She **inspired** flight and she **bore** fliers, but she herself—Belle La Follette—walked all her life on the ground to **keep the course** for her fliers. That was her woman's victory; that was a woman's tragedy, too."

Belle reading a letter by the light of a window in 1924.

Why did he say it was a tragedy? Perhaps it was because Belle lived during a time when many people still did not

inspired: encouraged   **bore**: gave birth to   **keep the course**: to make the way smooth

believe women were capable of achievements outside of the home. Belle had lived during a time of great change in society, especially in the lives of women. During her childhood, most people believed that a woman should stay home to take care of her children, support her husband, and manage the household. Toward the end of the 1800s, new chances to get an education, find better jobs, and fight for women's suffrage caused many women to question this role. As someone living through this change, Belle questioned women's roles but did not give up her role as wife and mother. Taking care of her family and looking after Bob's needs was always her first **priority**. But Belle also accomplished things most women of her time did not, such as getting a law degree, writing magazine columns, and fighting for important causes such as world peace and the vote for women.

Though she had accomplished many things, Belle wasn't well known for all of the work she had done outside the home. Bob's work had made him famous, but Belle's went unnoticed by many. Belle's **obituary** in the *New York Times* described her as "perhaps the least known, yet most

priority (prl **or** i tee): something that is more important than other things   **obituary** (oh **bi** choo air ee): a newspaper report of someone's death

107

influential of all the American women who have had to do with public affairs."

Bob has been best remembered for his political work. In Wisconsin, he is still remembered for his fiery speeches and stubborn politics. He is honored each year during Fighting Bob Fest, when people gather together

In 1929, Jo Davidson created this sculpture to honor Bob La Follette's legacy. Today, it sits in the United States Capitol in Washington, D.C.

to remember Wisconsin's most famous politician and to continue to shape Wisconsin's "Progressive" history.

VOTE PROGRESSIVE
"Keep Wisconsin Famous"
--PHIL LA FOLLETTE

WHI IMAGE ID 27276

A Progressive Party campaign poster from 1935.

After Bob died, the work he **pioneered** continued. His
sons, Bob Jr. and Phil, became well-known politicians and
reformers. They worked with other Wisconsin leaders to build
the Progressive Party, a political party that fought for reform
just as Fighting Bob had done during his lifetime. Many years
later, in 1959, Bob was honored by John F. Kennedy, a senator
who would later be president. Senator Kennedy named Bob La
Follette as one of the 5 greatest senators in U.S. history. Today,
you can see Bob's portrait in the lobby of the Senate building
in Washington, D.C.

The fact that Bob La Follette was considered such a
remarkable politician is a **tribute** to both his *and* Belle's
achievements. From their early days as students at college

pioneered: started, was the first to start   **tribute**: something done, given, or said to show thanks or respect

109

Belle Case La Follette, the
"ablest individual in the land."

"Fighting Bob" La Follette,
Wisconsin's progressive pioneer.

through their years as husband and wife and as political
leaders, they worked as partners to create a better world. Bob
trusted Belle's judgment. Belle admired Bob's courage. She
had faith in what he was doing, and she helped him to do it
well. Together, they devoted themselves to fighting for the
underprivileged and for peace.

In his later years, Bob would describe his years as
Wisconsin's governor as the time "when we were governor."

underprivileged (un dur **priv** lejd): lacking opportunities or advantages enjoyed by others

By "we," he meant both he and Belle. Belle felt the same way. In an interview in the *New York American* in 1924, Belle said, "I have loved my life. I have been fortunate, marvelously lucky in having all these years a **companion**. True companionship is the greatest thing in the world. We have been through everything, my husband and I, bad times and good times, disappointments, illness, poverty, hard work, the struggle for **principle**, the climb to success. But when you have a companion to count upon through thick and thin, it's all easy. We have kept together because—well, because our minds and our hearts are matched."

The world is a better place because of these extraordinary minds and hearts.

companion: someone with whom you spend time; a friend   **principle**: a basic law, truth, or belief

Appendix

Belle and Bob's Time Line

1855 — Robert Marion La Follette is born in Primrose, Wisconsin, on June 14.

1859 — Belle Case La Follette is born in Summit, Wisconsin, on April 21.

1859 — Bob starts school in Primrose at the age of 4.

1863–1875 — Belle attends school in Baraboo for 12 years.

1868–1870 — Bob attends school in Argyle, Wisconsin.

1873 — Bob moves to Madison to prepare for the University of Wisconsin.

1875 — Belle moves to Madison to attend the University of Wisconsin. She and Bob meet in their first-year German class.

1878 — Bob and Belle are engaged.

1879 — Belle receives an award for her graduation speech. Bob wins the Interstate Oratorical Contest. Both graduate from college.

Belle moves to Spring Green to teach high school. Bob begins law school at the University of Wisconsin.

1881 — Bob is elected district attorney of Dane County.

Belle Case and Bob La Follette marry on December 31.

1882 — Fola, Belle and Bob's first child, is born on September 10.

1883 — Belle enrolls in the University of Wisconsin Law School.

1884 — Bob La Follette is elected to Congress.

1885 — Belle is the first female to graduate from the University of Wisconsin Law School.

1886–1889 — Bob serves 2 more terms in Congress.

1890 — Bob loses his bid for re-election to Congress.

1894 — Belle organizes a fitness school in Madison.

1895 — Robert Marion La Follette Jr. is born on February 6.

1897 — Philip Fox La Follette is born on May 8.

1899 — Mary La Follette is born on August 16.

1900 — Bob is elected governor of Wisconsin on November 6.

1902 and 1904 — Bob is re-elected governor of Wisconsin.

1905 — Bob is elected to the U.S. Senate on January 25. He doesn't take his seat in Senate until 1906.

1907 — Bob's bill for workers' rights becomes law on January 10.

1909 — Belle and Bob start *La Follette's Weekly Magazine* on January 9.

1913 — Belle speaks before the Senate Committee on Woman Suffrage on April 26.

1915 — Belle attends the meeting at which the Woman's Peace Party is started in January.

1917 — Bob votes against the United States entering World War I.

1919 — On June 4, women gain the right to vote, a cause Belle fought hard for.

1920 — Belle leads a peace rally on Pennsylvania Avenue in Washington, D.C.

1924 — Bob loses the election for U.S. president, as candidate for the Progressive Party.

1925 — Bob Lafollette dies on June 18, and Bobbie (Robert Jr.) fills his vacant seat in the Senate.

1930 — Bob and Belle's son Phil becomes governor of Wisconsin.

1931 — Belle Case La Follette dies on August 18.

Glossary

Pronunciation Key

a cat (kat), plaid (plad), half (haf)

ah father (**fah** THur), heart (hahrt)

air carry (**kair** ee), bear (bair), where (whair)

aw all (awl), law (law), bought (bawt)

ay say (say), break (brayk), vein (vayn)

e bet (bet), says (sez), deaf (def)

ee bee (bee), team (teem), fear (feer)

i bit (bit), women (**wim** uhn), build (bild)

I ice (is), lie (li), sky (ski)

o hot (hot), watch (wotch)

oh open (**oh** puhn), sew (soh)

oi boil (boil), boy (boi)

oo pool (pool), move (moov), shoe (shoo)

or order (**or** dur), more (mor)

ou house (hous), now (nou)

u good (gud), should (shud)

uh cup (kuhp), flood (fluhd), button (**buht** uhn)

ur burn (burn), pearl (purl), bird (burd)

yoo use (yooz), few (fyoo), view (vyoo)

hw what (hwuht), when (hwen)

TH that (THat), breathe (breeTH)

zh measure (**mezh** ur), garage (guh **razh**)

abruptly (uh **brup** lee): suddenly

absorbed (uhb **zorbd**): taken in, understood

accumulated (uh **kyoom** yoo lay tud): gathered, piled up

aloft: high up in the air

approximate (uh **prok** si mayt): to come close to

arraigned (uh **raynd**): to ask someone accused of a crime whether he or she is guilty or not guilty

assassinated (uh **sa** si nay tud): killed because of fame or power

ballot: the vote

Balmoral (bahl **maw** ruhl): Scottish

bar: the group of lawyers allowed to practice law in a particular state

bar exam: a test to see whether someone is ready to be a lawyer

before: in front of

bellerin': slang for bellowing, to shout or yell

bill: a plan for a new law

bloomers: loose pants gathered at the knee, worn by women suffragettes to show their independence

boarding house: a house that provided meals and rooms for students living away from home

bore: gave birth to

bribe: money or gifts offered illegally to someone to persuade him or her to do something for you

brief: a paper that lists all the important facts about a court case

buggy: a carriage with 2 wheels, pulled by a horse

builds: believes in

campaign: a period of time before an election when candidates try to get voters to vote for them

campaigned (cam **paynd**): talked with people and gave speeches in order to get votes

cargo: goods that are carried by ship or airplane

Chautauqua (chuh **tawk** wah): a traveling education show with lectures, plays, and musical performances popular in the early 1900s

cherish (**chair** ish): to care for someone or something in a kind and loving way

chief justice: the highest judge in the supreme court

child labor: the use of children as workers in factories, farms, and mines

choice: well chosen, of good quality

citrus: orange, lime, or lemon

Civil War: the war between the Southern states and the Northern states, which lasted from 1861 to 1865

column (**kah** luhm): an article by the same person that appears regularly in a newspaper or magazine

companion: someone with whom you spend time; a friend

compel: to make someone do something

compensation: money a worker gets when he or she is hurt on the job

confidence: strong belief in oneself or one's abilities

conflict: a problem or disagreement between 2 things

constellation (kahn stuh **lay** shun): a group of stars that forms a shape or pattern

convention: a large gathering of people from the same political party

coral: a rock-hard substance found underwater, made up of the skeletons of tiny sea creatures

corruption (kuh **ruhp** shun): lack of honesty; willingness to accept bribes

corset: a close-fitting undergarment worn to support and shape the waistline, hips, and breasts

counsel: to give advice

covered wagon: a large, wooden wagon with a canvas cover spread over metal hoops, used by pioneers in the 1800s

decade (**dek** ayd): a period of 10 years

declare: to announce something formally

defended: supported, argued for

deign (dayn): to lower oneself

democracy (de **mok** ruh see): a system of government that allows people to choose their own candidates

depressed (dee **presd**): in a state of long-lasting unhappiness

depression (dee **pre** shun): a state of long-lasting unhappiness

determined (dee **tur** mind): absolutely sure

diaphragm (**dI** uh fram): the wall of muscle between the chest and the stomach

diploma: a certificate from a school showing that one has graduated

disarm: when a country gives up its weapons

disgrace: to cause shame or embarrassment

disposed: ready

disrespectful: lacking respect; rude

disrupting: disturbing or interrupting

distinguished (dis **ting** guishd): well known and respected

district attorney (**dis** trikt uh **tur** nee): the lawyer who puts people on trial for crimes in a city or county

dormitory: a building with many rooms for sleeping

draft: a law that requires men to fight in war

drawing: breathing in

dress: clothing

dueling (**doo** ling): formal combat between 2 persons to the death

dull: boring

editor: a person who decides what should go in a magazine or book

essay: a piece of writing about a particular subject

ethical: having to do with what is good and bad, and how people treat one another in groups

evaluate (ee **val** yoo ayt): to decide how good or valuable something is after thinking carefully about it

excited: brought about, sparked

expectations: hopes

fare: money paid to ride a train

fatigue (fuh **teeg**): great tiredness

fitness school: a school for exercise, popular in the late 1800s

freshman year: the first year of college

frontier: the far edge of a settled area, where few people live

furrow: the groove cut by a plow when it turns over the soil

gesture (**jes** chur): a movement that shows a feeling

glee club: a chorus of singers

governor (**guhv** uh nur): the person elected as the head of the state to represent all the people in the state

graduated (**graj** oo way tud): finished school

grievance (**gree** vins): reason to be angry

hollerin': slang for hollering, yelling loudly

hops: the dried, ripe flowers of the hop plant, which contains a bitter oil used in making beer

humble: not proud

independent: not Republican or Democrat

influence (**in** floo ens): to get someone to do something or to think in a certain way

inspiration (ins puh **ray** shun): something that encourages and influences someone to do something

inspired: encouraged

insult: to offend or hurt with words

involved: taking part in

junior year: the third year of college

keep the course: to make the way smooth

law school: a school one attends to learn to be a lawyer

lecture (**lek** shur): a talk given to an audience, often at a college or university

legislature (**lej** uhs lay chur): an elected group of people who have the power to make or change laws for a state or nation

lobby: to try to influence someone to vote a certain way

looking daggers: to glare at angrily

loyalty: faithful to one's country, family, friends, or beliefs

manage: to be in charge of something

medicinal (me **di** si nuhl): used to treat illness

menace (**men** is): a threat or danger

mentor: a wise and trusted counselor or teacher

militarism (mil i tur **i** zum): love of war

misapprehension (mis ap ree **hen** shun): not understanding

misquoted: incorrectly wrote down the words someone has said

motto: a short sentence that states what someone believes in or stands for

movement: a group of people who have joined together to support a cause

Napoleon (nuh **poh** lee uhn): a famous general who became the ruler of France at the end of the 1790s

nominated (**nah** mi nay tud): chosen to run in an election

nutrition: the science of healthy eating

obituary (oh **bi** choo air ee): a newspaper report of someone's death

office: a political job, such as governor, senator, or president

opposing: on opposite sides, disagreeing

oration (or **ay** shun): a memorized speech given in front of an audience

oratorical (or uh **tor** i kul): having to do with public speaking

patriotism: love for one's country

perish: disappear, die

persuasive (pur **sway** siv): good at giving reasons for someone to believe something

pioneered: started, was the first to start

platform: a set of beliefs of a political party on the important issues of the day

plead: to ask with great emotion

pneumonia (nuh **mohn** yuh): a disease that causes the lungs to be filled with fluid, making breathing difficult

pocketbook: a small case used to hold money

politician (pol uh **tish** un): someone who runs for or holds public office, such as a senator

politics: the way a city, state, or nation governs itself

pompadour (**pom** puh dor): a hairstyle in which the front hair is swept up from the forehead

population: the total number of people living in a certain place

position: in politics, a stance or view on a particular issue

poverty: the state of being poor

practical: useful in getting a task done

prairie (**prair** ee): a large area of flat or rolling grassland with few or no trees

prime: main

principle: a basic law, truth, or belief

priority (prI **or** i tee): something that is more important than other things

privy (prI vee): a toilet

progressive (proh **gres** iv): in favor of reform or improvement

Progressive Party: political party formed by Bob La Follete and his followers in the early 1900s to make positive changes in government, education, and rights

proper: strictly following rules, especially in behavior

proposed: asked someone to marry you

public affairs: issues that affect everybody, such as health or education

publisher: the person in charge of a magazine

racial equality (**ray** shul ee **kwah** li tee): people of all races having the same rights

rally: a gathering of a large group of people for a specific cause

recalled: remembered

recitation (re si **tay** shun): a speech that is memorized and performed

record: stand, stance

reform: changing something for the better

reformer: someone who wants to change things for the better

register: a vent for heating

regret: being sorry for something that happened in the past

reluctant: not wanting to do something

represents (rep ri **zents**): stands or acts for

Republican [ri **puhb** li kin] **Party and Democratic** [dem uh **kra** tik] **Party**: the 2 major American political parties, both now and in the past

reputation (rep yoo **tay** shun): your worth or character, as judged by other people

responsible: having important duties, being in charge

review: a piece of writing that gives an opinion about a new book, play, or movie

right: a thing you are allowed to do or have by law, such as going to school or being able to vote

scarce: hardly

scolding: reprimanding, punishing

scot-free: without being punished

scythe (sIth): a tool with a large curved blade used for cutting grass or crops by hand

sea urchin: a small sea creature with a soft body enclosed by a hard, spiny shell

segregation: the practice of keeping groups apart based on the color of their skin

senior year: the final year of college

Shetland ponies: a breed of ponies from the Shetland islands off the coast of Scotland, known for their small size

sideshow: a small performance that is part of a larger performance, such as at a circus

slogan: a phrase or motto

society: all the people who live in the same country and share the same laws or customs

solution: answer or remedy

sparked: started

spectator's gallery (**spec** tay torz **gal** uh ree): the balcony where an audience can watch representatives discuss laws

spellbound: on the edge of their seats

spring: a place where water rises up from underground and becomes a stream

stalling: delaying or pausing in order to have more time

state capital: the city where the state government is located

state representative: one of several people chosen to speak and act for the people of a state

stock: cows, horses, pigs, and other animals raised on a farm

strategy: a clever plan to achieve a goal

submitted: handed in

suffrage (**suhf** rij): the right to vote

suffragette (suf ruh **jet**): a woman who fought for the right to vote in the early 1900s

superhuman: beyond ordinary human ability

supporter: in politics, one who gives money to a candidate to help with a campaign

supreme: best, greatest

supreme court: the highest court of law in a state or nation, made up of several judges

suspicion: mistrust, doubt

term: in politics, the period of time one serves in an elected office

thereafter: after that

trade: a job that requires working with the hands or with machines

tradition: a way of life passed down from generation to generation

traitor: someone who aids the enemy of his or her country

tribute: something done, given, or said to show thanks or respect

trivial: unimportant

tuition (too **i** shun): money paid to take classes

unanimously (yoo **nan** i muhs lee): with everyone's agreement

underprivileged: lacking opportunities or advantages enjoyed by others

unwritten rule: a rule that is followed but not written down

ventilation: system that allows fresh air into a room and sends stale air out

villain: a wicked person, often an evil character in a play

vow: a serious and important promise

vowed: promised

work permit: a piece of paper signed by an official that gives someone permission to work

Reading Group Guide and Activities

Discussion Questions

🐾 Bob La Follette was famous for his honesty. List examples in this book of times when you think he acted with great honesty. Can you give examples of times when you were especially honest about something?

🐾 Although Belle was a gifted speaker and writer, she did not make public speeches or write for *La Follette's Weekly Magazine* until she was in her fifties. Why do you think she waited so long? What difficulties did Belle have to overcome to do these things? If she were alive today, how might her choices be different? Why?

🐾 Bob's stubborn positions sometimes got him into trouble. For example, he didn't think the United States should take part in World War I. However, his positions also were what made him famous, and gave him the nickname "Fighting Bob." Why was he admired for being stubborn? Do you admire his stubbornness? Why or why not?

🐾 The La Follette kids—Fola, Bobbie, Phil, and Mary—grew up surrounded by politics. What would it be like today to grow up the son or daughter of a famous politician? What expectations would your parents have? Would you want to follow in their footsteps or take a different path? Why or why not?

Activities

- Imagine that you are living in the 1850s and go to school in a one-room schoolhouse. What is different about going to school with all of the grades in one room and with just one teacher? What is the same? After you think through the differences, write a short story about a day in the life of a one-room schoolhouse.

- Bob La Follette was well known for his fiery, persuasive speeches. Belle was also a great public speaker, because she strongly believed in the causes she fought for. Think about an issue that you feel strongly about. Prepare a 2-minute speech about the cause of your choice to your classmates. Say what the cause is, why it is important, and what you think should be done about it.

- Imagine you are running in an election to represent your class to the whole school. It is your job to figure out what issues are most important to your classmates: cafeteria food, field trips, recess, etc. What is your position on the issues? What changes would you like to make? Create a list of things you will stand for as class representative, and what you will do to achieve them.

To Learn More about Politics

Giesecke, Ernestine. *State Government: Kid's Guide*. New York: Heineman, 2000.

Kasparek, John and Bobbie Malone. *Voices & Votes: How Democracy Works in Wisconsin*. Madison: Wisconsin Historical Society Press, 2005.

Krull, Kathleen. *A Kid's Guide to America's Bill of Rights: Curfews, Censorship, and the 100-Pound Giant*. New York: HarperCollins, 1999.

Maestro, Betsy and Guilio Maestro. *A More Perfect Union: The Story of Our Constitution*. New York, HarperCollins, 2008.

———. *The Voice of the People: American Democracy in Action*. New York: HarperCollins, 1996.

Sobel, Syl. *How the U.S. Government Works*. New York: Barron's Educational Series, 1999.

———. *Presidential Elections: And Other Cool Facts*. New York: Barron's Educational Series, 2001.

Acknowledgments

As a child, I first learned about politics and activism while watching my brothers, Ken and Mark, work to end the war in Vietnam. During my college years at the University of Wisconsin–Madison, Professors Harvey Goldberg and Booth Fowler deepened my interest in politics and my commitment to help right the wrongs of the world. Over the past few years, my son Shayle and many of his friends have shown me, to my great joy, that yet another generation of young people is dedicating its talents to solving the problems of the world. Bob and Belle La Follette's determination to fight for justice reminded me that activism did not begin with Vietnam and inspired me to write their story.

I am deeply grateful to the friends, family members, and staff of the Wisconsin Historical Society Press (WHSP), who edited early drafts of the La Follette's story and made invaluable suggestions. Caroline Hoffman helped me to blend the separate stories of Bob and Belle into one fluid tale. Deborah Waxman improved the grammar and style of the book page by page, and even word by word. Judy Landsman made this book more readable for children. Bobbie Malone, Director of the Office of School Services for the Wisconsin Historical Society, again provided me with the luxurious opportunity to work with WHSP and shared her insightful comments to ensure that history and storytelling were happily wed. Sara Philips, my editor at WHSP, added her own stamp and skillfully shaped the book into its present form. Jill Bremigan designed the cover and interior pages for the book. Thank you also to WHSP Production Editor Elizabeth Boone and to copyeditor Dawn Shoemaker for your fine attention to detail. Thank you all for your assistance.

⁊

This book is dedicated to political activists past, present, and future who continue to fight the good fight for Progressive politics in the spirit of Bob and Belle La Follette.

Following is a list of sources consulted while writing this book:

Freeman, Lucy, Sherry La Follette, and George Zabriske. *Belle: The Biography of Belle Case La Follette*. New York: Beaufort Books, 1986.

Kasparek, Jonathan. *Fighting Son: A Biography of Philip F. La Follette* Madison: Wisconsin Historical Society Press, 2006.

La Follette, Belle Case, and Fola La Follette. *Robert M. La Follette, June 14, 1855-June 18, 1925*. 2 vols. New York: Macmillan, 1953.

La Follette, Robert M. *La Follette's Autobiography: A Personal Narrative of Political Experiences*. Madison, The Robert M. La Follette Co., 1913.

Thelen, David. *The Early Life of Robert M. La Follette, 1855-1884*. Chicago: Loyola University Press, 1966.

———. *Robert La Follette and the Insurgent Spirit*. Boston: Little Brown and Company, 1976.

Unger, Nancy. *Fighting Bob La Follette: The Righteous Reformer*. Madison: Wisconsin Historical Society Press, 2008.

Weisberger, Bernard. *The La Follettes of Wisconsin*. Madison: University of Wisconsin Press, 1994.

Index

This index points you to the pages where you can read about persons, places, and ideas. If you do not find the word you are looking for, try to think of another word that means about the same thing.

When you see a page number in **bold** it means there is a picture on that page.